A Brief History of the Twentieth Century

A Brief History of the Twentieth Century

A GUIDE TO UNDERSTANDING THE
TWENTY-FIRST

———

Dr. Bradley W. Rasch

Table of Contents

Introduction

——

Is it possible to summarize an entire century by explaining the thirty most important events that occurred during that period of time? Can one look to the next century and understand it better by knowing the past?

Pearl S. Buck famously stated: "If you want to understand today, you have to search yesterday." James Baldwin Said, "People are trapped in history, and history is trapped in them."

Indeed, to see forward, we have to look back. This book will summarize thirty seminal events of the twentieth century, in an effort to understand the twenty-first.

CHAPTER 1

The Fall of the Iron Curtain

——

ON NOVEMBER 9, 1989 THE Berlin Wall fell. It had stood since 1961. Anti-communist revolutions across the continent culminated in ordinary people taking down the Berlin Wall piece by piece. The next year, the Soviet Union disintegrated into 15 countries.

The end of the "Cold War" potentially saved trillions of dollars and hundreds of thousands of lives. Perhaps the ending of this standoff saved humanity itself.

After World War II the United States and it's allies squared off against the Soviet Union and the countries it dominated separating the world into two competing and suspicious factions: NATO versus the Warsaw Pact. Those in the west perceived it as freedom versus liberty or good versus evil.

Though the United States and the Soviet Union never squared off directly during the Cold War, they often competed in proxy wars such as Korea, Vietnam, and even Afghanistan (when the Soviet Union was attempting to dominate them) from 1979 to 1989.

The end of the Cold War, the fall of the Berlin Wall, led to the lessening of tensions around the world, the reunification of Germany, and a sense of optimism unmatched during the twentieth Century.

A key figure in this event was Mikhail Gorbachev, the Soviet Union's last President (1989-1994) whose reforms led to the end of the Cold War.

Currently, economic and other pressures within Russia are causing the Russian President to revive, in a sense, the Cold War, to distract from his nations failing economy.

The legacy of this event in the current century is a resurgent Germany, a significant economic and moral power in the world. The end of the Cold War has had too many positive effects for it to be rekindled on a permanent basis to distract from any nations short-term difficulties (it is hoped).

CHAPTER 2

One Giant Leap for Mankind

———

JULY 20, 1969 NEIL ARMSTRONG was the first human to set foot on the moon. "One small step for (a) man, one giant leap for mankind." A giant leap it was indeed. This great scientific accomplishment came seven years after President Kennedy announced that the United States would accomplish this.

Certainly, this accomplishment was triggered by the Cold War competition between the United States and the Soviet Union. America had to respond to The 1957 Sputnik victory by the Soviet Union. The Cold War must be won.

The "space race" led to numerous scientific breakthroughs that paid extraordinary dividends in many fields. These breakthroughs more than justified the high costs of the space program.

Perhaps more importantly, the accomplishments of the space program and NASA developed a healthy respect for science, and a can-do optimism that has helped this country tackle many difficult challenges.

The legacy of the moon landing in the twenty-first century will be a support for science, a belief that the difficult can be accomplished with the proper funding and support, and an understanding that ambitious scientific goals can lead to significant and unforeseen advancements.

CHAPTER 3

The Holocaust

———

THE HOLOCAUST OCCURRED DURING WORLD War II. Responsible was the Nazi regime of Germany. It was perpetrated against Jewish citizens for the most part, but it should be remembered that the physically and mentally disabled, homosexuals, other religious groups and ethnicities were also targeted. The Holocaust has become synonymous with genocide.

Over six million Jews were killed during this attempt of genocide. This amounted to 80 percent of the European Jewish population.

Why did the Holocaust occur? It was a state-sponsored murder spree of people deemed a threat to the regime. Good people looked away.

What impact has the Holocaust had on the current century?

1. The international community has and will focus more on human rights, especially of minority and persecuted populations.
2. Genocide, or calls for it, are recognized and not ignored as "local" issues.
3. Israel is viewed internationally by many nations as a sanctuary for a population that has historically been persecuted.
4. Germany has become a force for good in terms of assisting persecuted groups, European cooperation, and inter-religious and inter-ethnic cooperation.

CHAPTER 4

Charles Lindbergh and the Spirit of St. Louis

——

A TWENTY-FIVE YEAR OLD AIRMAIL pilot, Charles Lindbergh, sought a $25,000 prize offered by hotelier Raymond Orteig. To win the prize, one had to fly non-stop from New York to Paris.

Lindbergh found some sponsors, and helped design the aircraft himself. The plane, the spirit of St. Louis, was named after some financial backers in St. Louis.

Lindbergh took off on May 20, 1927 and landed in Paris 40 hours later.

His flight was successful. One cannot overestimate Lindbergh's celebrity and influence after this historic flight. His effort prompted transoceanic travel, an acceptance of air travel, and was a first real step in making the world seem like a smaller place.

What is often forgotten is that this young man made history before the flight over the Atlantic. Prior to the flight to Paris, he flew the plane from San Diego, where it was built, to New York. This transcontinental flight encouraged long distance flights within the United States, and was quite an accomplishment in it's own right.

Long distance flights continue to be important for trade and cultural reasons and will continue to be for the foreseeable future.

CHAPTER 5

The Spanish Flu Pandemic

—

PANDEMIC, IN RELATION TO A disease, is defined as prevalent throughout an entire country, continent, or the whole world; epidemic over a large area. The Spanish Flu Pandemic of 1918 to 1920 certainly adheres to this definition.

We still do not know where the Spanish Flu began. It appeared in North America, Asia, and Europe at the same time. The disease spread exponentially because of World War I. Troops were being transported around the world and carried the disease with them. It is thought that about one third of the world's population contracted this disease, and up to 100 million died form it, far more deaths than combat casualties during the first World War. Because the World was at war, quarantines were usually not put into effect as troops had to be moved. This exasperated this serious health emergency.

Soldiers in close quarters during the war facilitated the spread of this disease.

Recently, we have learned one of histories great pandemics was a variant of what we now call the H1N1 virus.

Pandemics will always occur. What we have learned from the Spanish Flu Pandemic of 1918-1920 is the importance of quarantine and control measures.

CHAPTER 6

The Double Helix

———

IN 1953 JAMES WATSON, FRANCIS Crick, and Maurice Wilkins were recognized as the first to understand the structure of deoxyribonucleic acid (DNA). The discovery of this double helix structure led to a greater understanding of genetics. Lost in history are Friedrich Miescher, a Swiss scientist, that discovered DNA in the 1800's and Rosalind Franklin whose work that took place at the same time as that of Watson, Crick, and Wilkins, was just as important. Franklin, being a woman, was not given the recognition she deserved. Watson, Crick, and Wilkins shared the Nobel Prize in 1962.

The discovery of the Double Helix, and the increased understanding of genetics, made science important in the public mind. Scientists became celebrities just like astronauts, test pilots, and athletes.

What is important is the discovery, not so much who is given credit for it. Understanding DNA has led to improved understanding of and treatment for diseases. Scientists continue to be viewed as heroic, and funding for scientific research has, and will continue to be, a priority.

CHAPTER 7

"The Pill"

———

GREGORY PINCUS, A BIOLOGIST, RECEIVED funding from a wealthy philanthropist, Katherine McCormick; to fund his research intended to develop an oral contraceptive for women. With others, Pincus developed what is now simply called "the pill'.

The control that women gained over their fertility gave them much more control over their private and professional lives. This control had been lacking up to that point in time.

Though the use of oral contraceptives remains controversial to some, they are not going away anytime soon.

Prior to 1965, oral contraceptives were illegal in many states. In 1965 the *Supreme Court of the United States decided the Griswold v. Connecticut case*. This case prohibited states from banning birth control pills to married couples. In 1972, the right to birth control pills was extended to unmarried women by *Eisenstadt v Baird*.

The impact of the pill on a modern society cannot be over stated.

CHAPTER 8

The End of Smallpox

IN 1980 THE WORLD HEALTH Organization declared smallpox eradicated. The last smallpox death occurred in 1978 in the UK due to a lab accident. Both the United States and Russia have maintained supplies of lab specimens of this deadly disease.

Prior to its eradication, smallpox may have been the biggest killer in human history. During the twentieth century, it is thought that smallpox killed as many as 500 million people.

A scourge throughout history was quickly eradicated by human beings cooperating. In 1956 the World Health Organization committed to ending the disease. It was eradicated by 1980.

As a species, when we put our mind to it, we can use science and cooperate to confront our largest challenges.

CHAPTER 9

The Long March

———

CHINA WAS IN THE THROES of a great civil war in 1934. Mao Zedong led a group of communist rebels against the government of Chiang Kai-Shek, a leader preferred by the United States. From 1934 to 1935 Mao led his rebels, numbering about 100,000 on a 6,000-mile march across China to a safe haven where they could not be destroyed by government forces. Though the Long March saved the communist rebels from eradication by the government, the Chinese government was distracted by an invasion from Japan, and gave the conflict against the Japanese priority.

Mao and the communists eventually gained control in China, thus changing the course of the worlds most populace nation and the world itself.

CHAPTER 10

Martin Luther King's Dream

———

MARTIN LUTHER KING, JR. DID much to bring greater equality to America and to guarantee civil rights for its entire people regardless of their race. The important things that Martin Luther King did were to:

1. Bring attention to major civil rights activities and efforts
2. Made sure his movement emphasized non-violence
3. Led the civil rights movement for African-Americans

Martin Luther King, Jr. was a well-known civil rights leader and activist who had a great deal of influence on American society in the 1950s and 1960s. His legacy lives on today. His strong belief in non-violent protest helped set the tone of the American civil rights movement. Boycotts, protests, and marches were eventually effective, and much legislation was passed against racial discrimination.

Assassinated in 1968, King's life was filled with many great accomplishments, in which he worked to promote the equal treatment of all races; his non-violent approach to protesting, his followers, and his true belief in the ability of mankind to live in peace went a long way toward advancement of civil rights during that tumultuous time in American history.

King's accomplishments are many. Some of his major achievements included:

*   Being an advocate for nonviolent protest in the Memphis sanitation worker strike. This demonstrated his concern for the disadvantaged of all races.
*   Providing leadership in the Montgomery bus boycott of 1955

- His famous "I Have a Dream" speech
- Being instrumental in establishing the Southern Christian Leadership Conference (SCLC) in 1957, which was a civil rights organization that supported the philosophy of non-violence

In 1968 1,300 black sanitation workers in Memphis, Tennessee were protesting terrible working conditions, discrimination, and lower pay. It was obvious they were discriminated against when they were sent home without pay while white workers stayed on the job.

They started a strike on February 12, 1968. Martin Luther King came to Memphis to speak and support the second march of the sanitation workers.

The strike lasted for 64 days and grew into one of the major civil rights events. The American Federation of State, County, and Municipal Employees (AFSCME) and the sanitation workers demanded an end to discrimination, higher wages, and union recognition. This attracted the national news media as well as others who joined the cause, like community leaders and members of the clergy. The strike finally ended on April 12, 1968, and the city of Memphis agreed to the workers' demands, even though more strikes had to be threatened to make them honor the agreement.

In Montgomery, Alabama, King led a boycott against city buses that refused to let blacks sit in the front seats of the bus. The protest gained followers rapidly, and it led to a citywide boycott of the bus system until the rules were changed; ultimately, after King and his followers were sent to jail, the boycott did succeed, and the unfair, racist law allowing the segregation aboard the buses was changed. This was a great success for the civil rights movement of the time, and gained national attention.

In 1963, Dr. King and other leaders of the civil rights movement organized a huge march for equal rights in Washington, DC. With a massive crowd of over 200,000 followers, the march was protesting racial discrimination in employment, racial separatism in schools, and they demanded minimum wage for all workers. It was the largest gathering in Washington, DC's history, and the site of King's most famous speech, "I Have a Dream."

As a result of the march and the speech, the citizens of the nation began to put growing pressure on the presidential administration of John F. Kennedy, encouraging the president to push for civil rights laws to pass through Congress and become recognized on a national level.

Because of his commitment to peace, non-violence and equality for all, King's protests on behalf of civil rights were able to make genuine headway in American society and allowed Martin Luther King to contribute a great deal to the success of the civil rights movement.

Even as his oppressors exercised force and brutality, King's insistence on avoiding violence, which he also taught his followers to practice, was a major factor in the respect and acknowledgment given to the civil rights movement during a time of unrest and unease in the country. His genuine desire for the country to come together was ultimately recognized as a great contribution to America; his untimely death was a loss to everyone and started an era of great potential for the nation.

This movement lasted from around 1955 to 1968. Its goals were to abolish racial discrimination in many areas including public transportation, employment, voting, and education.

Non-violent protests and civil disobedience during this time caused many crisis situations where the government had to take action. These showed the inequities and injustice that was happening to Blacks. The protests were done with sit-ins, marches, and boycotts. Notable legislation during this time included the:

- Civil Rights Act of 1964 - This banned discrimination in employment and public accommodations based on "race, color, religion, or national origin".
- Voting Rights Act of 1965 - This act restored and protected the right to vote.
- Immigration and Nationality Services Act of 1965 - This allows immigration from groups other than those from the traditional European countries.
- Fair Housing Act of 1968 - This banned housing discrimination for sales or rentals.

The civil rights movement was concerned with the basics of dignity, respect, freedom, and equality.

The following is the text of Dr. Martin Luther Kings "I had a Dream" speech, delivered from the steps of the Lincoln Memorial in Washington, DC.

Most historians consider it one of the greatest and most important speeches in American history.

"I am happy to join with you today in what will go down in history as the greatest demonstration for freedom in the history of our nation.

Five score years ago, a great American, in whose symbolic shadow we stand today, signed the Emancipation Proclamation. This momentous decree came as a great beacon light of hope to millions of Negro slaves who had been seared in the flames of withering injustice. It came as a joyous daybreak to end the long night of their captivity.

But one hundred years later, the Negro still is not free. One hundred years later, the life of the Negro is still sadly crippled by the manacles of segregation and the chains of discrimination. One hundred years later, the Negro lives on a lonely island of poverty in the midst of a vast ocean of material prosperity. One hundred years later, the Negro is still languished in the corners of American society and finds himself an exile in his own land. And so we've come here today to dramatize a shameful condition.

In a sense we've come to our nation's capital to cash a check. When the architects of our republic wrote the magnificent words of the Constitution and the Declaration of Independence, they were signing a promissory note to which every American was to fall heir. This note was a promise that all men, yes, black men as well as white men, would be guaranteed the "unalienable Rights" of "Life, Liberty and the pursuit of Happiness." It is obvious today that America has defaulted on this promissory note, insofar as her citizens of color are concerned. Instead of honoring this sacred obligation, America has given the Negro people a bad check; a check, which has come back, marked "insufficient funds."

But we refuse to believe that the bank of justice is bankrupt. We refuse to believe that there are insufficient funds in the great vaults of opportunity of this nation. And so, we've come to cash this check, a check that will give us upon demand the riches of freedom and the security of justice.

We have also come to this hallowed spot to remind America of the fierce urgency of Now. This is no time to engage in the luxury of cooling off or to take the tranquilizing drug of gradualism. Now is the time to make real the promises of democracy. Now is the time to rise from the dark and desolate valley of segregation to the sunlit path of racial justice. Now is the time to lift our nation from the quicksand of racial injustice to the solid rock of brotherhood. Now is the time to make justice a reality for all of God's children.

It would be fatal for the nation to overlook the urgency of the moment. This sweltering summer of the Negro's legitimate discontent will not pass until there is an invigorating autumn of freedom and equality. Nineteen sixty-three is not an end, but a beginning. And those who hope that the Negro needed to blow off steam and will now be content will have a rude awakening if the nation returns to business as usual. And there will be neither rest nor tranquility in America until the Negro is granted his citizenship rights. The whirlwinds of revolt will continue to shake the foundations of our nation until the bright day of justice emerges.

But there is something that I must say to my people, who stand on the warm threshold, which leads into the palace of justice: In the process of gaining our rightful place, we must not be guilty of wrongful deeds. Let us not seek to satisfy our thirst for freedom by drinking from the cup of bitterness and hatred. We must forever conduct our struggle on the high plane of dignity and discipline. We must not allow our creative protest to degenerate into physical violence. Again and again, we must rise to the majestic heights of meeting physical force with soul force.

The marvelous new militancy which has engulfed the Negro community must not lead us to a distrust of all white people, for many of our white brothers, as evidenced by their presence here today, have come to realize that their destiny is tied up with our destiny. And they have come to realize that their freedom is inextricably bound to our freedom.

We cannot walk alone.

And as we walk, we must make the pledge that we shall always march ahead. We cannot turn back.

There are those who are asking the devotees of civil rights, "When will you be satisfied?" We can never be satisfied as long as the Negro is the victim of the unspeakable horrors of police brutality. We can never be satisfied as long as our bodies, heavy with the fatigue of travel, cannot gain lodging in the motels of the highways and the hotels of the cities. *We cannot be satisfied as long as the negro's basic mobility is from a smaller ghetto to a larger one. We can never be satisfied as long as our children are stripped of their self-hood and robbed of their dignity by signs stating: "For Whites Only."* We cannot be satisfied as long as a Negro in Mississippi cannot vote and a Negro in New York believes he has nothing for which to vote. No, no, we are not satisfied, and we will not be satisfied until "justice rolls down like waters, and righteousness like a mighty stream."[1]

I am not unmindful that some of you have come here out of great trials and tribulations. Some of you have come fresh from narrow jail cells. And some of you have come from areas where your quest -- quest for freedom left you battered by the storms of persecution and staggered by the winds of police brutality. You have been the veterans of creative suffering. Continue to work with the faith that unearned suffering is redemptive. Go back to Mississippi, go back to Alabama, go back to South Carolina, go back to Georgia, go back to Louisiana, go back to the slums and ghettos of our northern cities, knowing that somehow this situation can and will be changed.

Let us not wallow in the valley of despair, I say to you today, my friends.

And so even though we face the difficulties of today and tomorrow, I still have a dream. It is a dream deeply rooted in the American dream.

I have a dream that one day this nation will rise up and live out the true meaning of its creed: "We hold these truths to be self-evident, that all men are created equal."

I have a dream that one day on the red hills of Georgia, the sons of former slaves and the sons of former slave owners will be able to sit down together at the table of brotherhood.

I have a dream that one day even the state of Mississippi, a state sweltering with the heat of injustice, sweltering with the heat of oppression, will be transformed into an oasis of freedom and justice.

I have a dream that my four little children will one day live in a nation where they will not be judged by the color of their skin but by the content of their character.

I have a *dream* today!

I have a dream that one day, down in Alabama, with its vicious racists, with its governor having his lips dripping with the words of "interposition" and "nullification" -- one day right there in Alabama little black boys and black girls will be able to join hands with little white boys and white girls as sisters and brothers.

I have a *dream* today!

I have a dream that one day every valley shall be exalted, and every hill and mountain shall be made low, the rough places will be made plain, and the crooked places will be made straight; "and the glory of the Lord shall be revealed and all flesh shall see it together."[2]

This is our hope, and this is the faith that I go back to the South with.

With this faith, we will be able to hew out of the mountain of despair a stone of hope. With this faith, we will be able to transform the jangling discords of our nation into a beautiful symphony of brotherhood. With this faith, we will be able to work together, to pray together, to struggle together, to go to jail together, to stand up for freedom together, knowing that we will be free one day.

And this will be the day -- this will be the day when all of God's children will be able to sing with new meaning:

My country 'tis of thee, sweet land of liberty, of thee I sing.
Land where my fathers died, land of the Pilgrim's pride,
From every mountainside, let freedom ring!

And if America is to be a great nation, this must become true.
And so let freedom ring from the prodigious hilltops of New Hampshire.
Let freedom ring from the mighty mountains of New York.
Let freedom ring from the heightening Alleghenies of Pennsylvania.
Let freedom ring from the snow-capped Rockies of Colorado.
Let freedom ring from the curvaceous slopes of California.

But not only that:
Let freedom ring from Stone Mountain of Georgia.
Let freedom ring from Lookout Mountain of Tennessee.
Let freedom ring from every hill and molehill of Mississippi.
From every mountainside, let freedom ring.

And when this happens, and when we allow freedom ring, when we let it ring from every village and every hamlet, from every state and every city, we will be able to speed up that day when *all* of God's children, black men and white men, Jews and Gentiles, Protestants and Catholics, will be able to join hands and sing in the words of the old Negro spiritual:

Free at last! Free at last!
Thank God Almighty, we are free at last!"

Dr. King's methods were admired throughout the world, as was he. His influence was felt worldwide, not just in the United States.

CHAPTER 11

The Stonewall

———

CENTERED AROUND THE STONEWALL INN on Christopher Street in New York City, the Stonewall riots between the New York police department and members of the New York metro area Lesbian/Gay/Bisexual/Transgender (LGBT) community began. The Stonewall riots are considered as the worldwide impetus for the modern LGBT rights movement. What exactly was Stonewall and what is its significance?

Stonewall was not the first time gay rights had been taken up, in fact the struggle had been fought unsuccessfully for some twenty years primarily led by Harry Hay and the Mattachine Society he founded. The Mattachine society's formation along with the Daughters of Bilitis (A lesbian society) founded in 1955 led to the formation of the of the first student gay rights organization founded by bisexual student Stephen Donaldson in 1967 at Colombia University called the Student Homophile League (SHL). In 1968, Jerald Moldenhaurer founded a second SHL at Cornell University. What this has to do with Stonewall is that it all set the tone for Stonewall and provided a large pool of demonstrators for the Stonewall rebellion/riots. Had these organizations have not existed and thrived in the New York region, the rebellion may likely have never carried forward.

To understand what life was like for an LGBT person in 1960's New York City (Or anywhere, for that matter) you must understand what daily life was like. Being closeted (Not publicly known as a homosexual or transgender person) was generally the only way to safely navigate life. Until the mid 1960's raids on gay establishments were a part of weekly life along with the shakedowns of owners and patrons known as "gayola." In fact in New York

City and many other cities across the United States it was not legal to serve an alcoholic beverage to a table in which three known homosexuals were seated together. Failure to comply would result in a fine and the closing of the establishment for the remainder of the business day. Consider that. For the LGBT person in question they could face a fine, an overnight stay in lockup, and often had their name printed in the daily newspapers police blotter along with a record of their "criminal" activity, thus ending their careers. So vigilant were the police in carrying out this task they often arrested patrons of gay establishments for indecency charges which may mean nothing more than the person was a cross dresser, seen kissing, dancing, or even holding hands with a same sex person. Generally just being there was enough in their minds to warrant arrest. When this appeared in the newspaper they were tabbed as having committed a "Crime against nature." Many lives were ruined in this manner.

By 1969 gay life in NYC had improved somewhat as the police began laying off the LGBT community establishments and set in house rules in place concerning the entrapment of gay men. However mayoral candidate John Lindsay was fighting a losing re-election battle and took a gamble that a campaign based on morals would get him back over the top. He saw the Stonewall was a prime target to focus on as it was frequented by a crowd made up primarily of blacks and Hispanics, many of whom were transgendered or drag queens which would appease the straight white male voter base he was courting. Police deputy inspector Seymour Pine felt that a number of thefts on Wall Street were directly linked to gay men who frequented the nearby Stonewall Inn. His reasoning for this was questionable at best as he assumed the thefts were gay men trying to pay off blackmailers to protect their secret. That was the extent of his investigation and speculative powers. Satisfied with this scenario, Lindsay gave the order to ""take down" the Stonewall Inn.

The raid itself was June 28, 1969 at 1:20 A.M. This raid was unlike others that the Stonewall or most any bar had faced before in that the police carried a warrant to investigate underage alcohol sales and not the usual morals clause violations concerning homosexuals. Eight officers arrived unlike the normal two, and of those only one was uniformed. Each patron was identified, mostly logged in the police officers notes, and questioned before being led outside or arrested. For the most part white male patrons were simply let go without having their name logged. Those arrested were the staff along with three drag queens and two male to female transsexuals. Onlookers began making catcalls aimed at the police. As the arrested parties were led to the paddy wagon they began resisting. Many believe a transgender person carried out the first action taken against the police although nobody can seem to exactly remember.

Officers were pelted with bottles and rocks, but what really sent things over the edge was when singer Dave van Ronk, a heterosexual that just happened to be passing by was dragged off the street and into the Stonewall where NYPD officers beat him. Word spread up and down the street and increased the number of demonstrators. Police would disperse the crowd only to see it grow even bigger. Eventually when the police re-entered the bar the angry mob blockaded them in and torched the Stonewall Inn.

Police detained a few particularly violent protesters but there were simply too many to deal with. Some protesters chanted "Gay Power" while others repeated the refrain:

> We are Stonewall girls
> We wear our hair in curls
> We wear no underwear
> We show our pubic hair
> We wear our dungarees
> Above our Nelly knees

Throughout the riots a number of transgender people along with those labeled as gender non-conformist's (Butch lesbians and effeminate men) were singled out from the crowd, beaten, and then arrested. On the first night there were thirteen arrests, and an unknown number of injuries. With the battle tipping the scales at two thousand protesters versus four hundred police officers, the NYPD sent in the Tactical Patrol Force (the Riot squad). Unable to disperse the crowd, the riot went on into the morning and resumed for four more nights.

While the Stonewall Inn shut down it's legacy lives on. This occasion led to the first instance of all factions of the LGBT uniting, gays, lesbians, bisexuals, and most notably the often-overlooked transgender community.

It was not until the twenty- fifth anniversary of Stonewall that Gay Pride organizing committees saw fit to include the transgender community in the remembrance of that day, a day in which they were the primary targets for arrests. The Stonewall Riots led to the formation of many gay rights groups, most notably the Gay Liberation Front, and the annual commemoration of the event led to today's Gay Pride Parades held every June around the world.

Remembering the Stonewall helps us remember those that took a stand for human equality and continue the struggle for not only those and ourselves in the future, but for those who lived in the dark days before us.

CHAPTER 12

JFK and the Cuban Missle Crisis

———

THE CUBAN MISSILE CRISIS WAS one of the few times that the generally accepted 'rules' of the Cold War were not obeyed. With the crisis Berlin, Hungary, Korea and the Suez– the 'rules' had been adhered to. But in Cuba, this broke down and the Cuban Missile Crisis was the only time when a real hot war could have broken out.

In the 1950's Cuba was lead by a right-wing dictator named Batista. He dealt with opponents with extreme harshness and while some prospered under his regime, many Cubans were very poor. He was not tolerant of communists and received the support of the United States. Batista's sole support within Cuba came from the army, which was equipped by the Americans.

Havana, the capital of Cuba, had been the play ground of the rich and famous from America. They would come to the island weekends to gamble – illegal in all parts of America except for Las Vegas at the time. Havana was considered more convenient for those living in the southern states of America. Large sums of money were spent but Batista and his cronies skimmed off most. Over $200 million was actually invested in Cuba itself. For all the money coming into Cuba, the poor remained very poor.

Some young Cubans, who had read about socialism and what it offered the poor, reacted against Batista's corruption. Their first attempt to overthrow the government was a failure and the small group of rebels fled to the Sierra Mastra – a remote area of Cuba. Here they sharpened their tactics and used the most valuable weapon they had, educating the oppressed in their ways. They used the tactics of Mao Tse Tung by actually helping out the peasants on their land. These people had been used to abuse for years and here were young educated people actually helping them for free.

It was only a matter of time before the 'message' spread to other areas of Cuba and by 1959, the rebels lead by **Fidel Castro** felt strong enough to overthrow the government of Batista. This they easily achieved as they were aided by popular support.

Castro's first task was to punish those who had abused the poor. Those found guilty were executed. He then nationalized all American firms in Cuba so that their wealth would be invested in Cuba itself rather than leave the island and go to multi-nationals in the United States. The money made from this measure was primarily spent on a national health system so that all-medical treatment was free and on education. Castro also introduced major land reforms.

Some Cubans fled and went to live in Florida. Many of their descendents today are strongly anti-Castro. These Cuban exiles were treated by some Americans as heroes and brought with them stories that outraged the American press. Many were false or exaggerated. America reacted by refusing any trade with Cuba. This trade embargo would have bankrupted the island as her biggest money earner was exporting sugar to America. Up to this time, there is little evidence that Castro or Cuba had any real intention of teaming up with communist Russia. In 1960, Castro referred to himself as a socialist – not a communist.

However, the trade embargo brought the two together as Russia stepped in to buy Cuba's sugar and other exports. The actions of America appear to have driven Castro into the support offered by Russia.

Now with a supporter of communism only a few miles from Florida, the new young American president – J F K– decided to give support to the anti-Castro Cubans who had gone to Florida. With CIA funding, a group of armed Cuban exiles tried to land in Cuba at the **Bay of Pigs** in 1961 with the sole intention of overthrowing the Castro government. It proved a fiasco – jeeps landed without fuel, no maps of the island being issued, Cuban exiles firing on Cuban exiles. But to Castro, this episode showed him where America stood in relations to Cuba. Kennedy did not apologize for America's involvement in this event.

After the Bay of Pigs debacle, Cuba obviously felt threatened by her massively powerful neighbor. Castro started to look for a closer relationship with Russia who could offer her protection.

In Sept 1962, anti-Castro Cuban refugees reported to the CIA that there was a build-up of Russian bases in Cuba.

On **October 16th 1962**, a U2 spy plane took high-level photographs over Cuba and the resulting photographic prints revealed what was obviously a base for missiles. These were later identified as being inter-mediate range missiles capable of carrying a nuclear payload.

On **October 17th 1962** the CIA reported to the president that the 16 to 32 missiles identified could kill 80 million Americans as they had a range of 2000 miles with a flight time of just 16 minutes. While this was happening, American Intelligence reported that over 20 Russian ships were heading for Cuba with crates on board that probably contained more missiles. They were not difficult to detect as they were being carried on deck in full view of US surveillance planes.

On **October 25th 1962** more U2 photographs showed that the bases would be fully operational in a few days – at the latest by the end of October.

The threat to USA was very obvious. On October 27th the matter was made worse when a Russian missile shot down a U2 and the pilot killed.

In total, the Russians sent 42 medium range missiles and 24 intermediate range missiles – which had a range of 3500 miles. 22,000 Russian troops and technicians accompanied the missiles.

What should Kennedy do?

He had already made a major mistake with the Bay of Pigs affair – now he could afford no such errors, as the consequences would be disastrous for everyone.

He had essentially five choices............

1. **He could do nothing and ignore the missiles. This would have been political suicide and if the Russians had seen this as weakness on his part, they could have taken advantage of it.**
2. **He could order a full-scale military invasion of Cuba. This could lead to heavy US casualties and that would be politically**

damaging. It would almost certainly involve Russian casualties, which could escalate the problem. The American chiefs-of-staff were not convinced that it would be successful either especially as the offending missile bases were in remote areas and most were well inland.

3. He could order an air strike against the missile bases only. The problem again would be Russian casualties and the Air Force was not sure it could deliver pin-point bombing raids on what were relatively small targets.

4. He could call on the Russians to remove the missiles explaining the damage their presence was doing to Russian/American relations. However, the Russians were highly unlikely to listen to a 'polite' request especially as they even refused to recognize the existence of the missiles at the United Nations emergency meeting on the matter.

5. He could put a naval blockade around the island quarantine it – and not allow any more Russian ships to Enter Cuba. This would still leave missiles on Cuba but the negotiations would continue in the background while public ally Kennedy would be seen to be doing something specific.

Following American protests, Khrushchev, the Russian leader, sent Kennedy two letters both of which sent conflicting messages.

One letter said that the missiles would be withdrawn if Kennedy promised not to invade Cuba.

The other was more threatening claiming that as USA had bases actually in Turkey, why should not the USSR have bases in Cuba especially as the people of Cuba wanted them? Khrushchev said that if United States removed missiles from Turkey then the USSR would remove them from Cuba. These messages left Kennedy confused.

Kennedy decided to act on Khrushchev's first letter and offered the following:

USSR was to remove its missiles from Cuba and USA was to end Cuba's quarantine and to give out a promise not to invade Cuba.

If the USSR did not respond by October 29th, USA would launch a military invasion of Cuba. On October 28th, Khrushchev replied that the USSR would remove the missiles. Within 2 months they were gone. The Cuban Missile Crisis was over but it had taken the world to the brink of nuclear war.

The end result of the crisis was seen as a huge success for Kennedy but contributed to the downfall of Khrushchev in Russia. The one positive thing to come out of the crisis was the creation of a hotline between Moscow and Washington to allow for easier communication between the two nations leaders at a time of crisis.

This is one of the few examples of the cold war where the two principle countries actually got involved themselves against the other. Up to 1962, other nations fought out the Cold War on their behalf (USA + China in Korea; USA + North Vietnamese in the Vietnam War etc.), as each knew that a conflict between the two would have the potential to be horrific.

The lessons learned from Cuba ensured that neither would push each to the brink again and that the 'rules' of the Cold War would be adhered to.

Just one year later in 1963, both nations signed the Nuclear Test Ban Treaty. This treaty stated that neither would explode nuclear bombs during testing in the atmosphere. This was a popular treaty in America and a sign that something positive had come out of the Cuban Crisis – that of a greater respect for each other.

CHAPTER 13

Henry Ford's Model T

_____

FROM 1908 TO 1927 THE Ford Motor Company produced the Model T in Detroit, Michigan. Ford applied assembly line techniques to automobile production so well that he was able to produce a Model T every 33 minutes. At one point in the 1920's, half of the cars in the entire world were Ford Model T's (Not all of them were made in Detroit, Ford built factories worldwide). Eventually, over 15,000,000 "Tin Lizzies" were manufactured.

Applying assembly line techniques allowed for efficiencies that significantly lowered the price of the automobile to the point where most people could afford to own a car, thus changing the landscape of not only America, but also the world. Motels, roads, drive-inns, all came about as a result of increased auto ownership. Suburbs would not have come into existence without the resultant mobile population.

Unfortunately, our dependence on and use of petroleum not only makes our nation reliant on other countries oil, but has impacted our environment significantly.

CHAPTER 14

The Wall Street Crash

———

THE 1929 CRASH OF THE Stock Market was a result of many economic imbalances and system failings. Here are some of the most significant economic factors behind the stock market crash of 1929:

During the "Roaring Twenties", there was a rapid growth in bank credit and bank loans. Encouraged by the strength of the economy the people felt the stock market was a sure bet. Some consumers borrowed significant sums of money to buy shares of stock. Firms took out more and more loans for expansion. Because people became highly in debt, it meant they became more susceptible to a change in confidence in the economy. When that change of confidence came in 1929, those who had borrowed were particularly exposed and joined the rush to sell their shares and try and redeem their debts.

Related to buying on credit was the practice of buying shares "on the margin". This meant you only had to pay 10 or 20% of the value of the shares; it meant you were borrowing 80-90% of the value of the shares. This enabled more money to be put into shares, increasing their value. It is said there were many 'margin millionaire' investors. These investors had made giant profits by buying on the margin and seeing share prices rise. However, it left investors very exposed when stock prices fell. These margin millionaires were wiped out when the stock market fall came. It also affected those banks and investors who had lent money to those buying on the margin.

A great deal of the Stock Market crash can be blamed on "over exuberance" and false expectations. In the years leading up to 1929, the stock market offered the potential for making huge gains in wealth. It was, in effect, the new gold rush. People bought shares with the expectations of making more and more money. As share prices rose, people started to borrow money to invest in the stock market. The market got caught up in a "speculative bubble." – Shares kept rising and people felt they would continue to do so. The problem was that stock prices became separated from the real potential earnings of the share prices. Prices were not being driven by economic fundamentals but the over optimism / over exuberance of investors. The average earning per share rose by 400% between 1923 and 1929. Yet, those who questioned the value of shares were often perceived as "doom-mongers".

This was not the first investment bubble the nation experienced, nor was it the last. Most recently we saw a similar phenomena in the dot.com bubble.

In March 1929, the stock market saw its first major reverse, but this mini-panic was overcome leading to a strong rebound in the summer of 1929. By October 1929, shares were significantly overvalued. When some companies posted disappointing results on October 24 (Black Thursday), some investors started to feel this would be a good time to cash in on their profits; share prices began to fall and panic selling caused prices to fall sharply. Financiers, such as JP Morgan tried to restore confidence by buying shares to prop up prices. This failed to alter the rapid change in market sentiment. On October 29(Black Tuesday) share prices fell by $40 billion in a single day. By 1930 the value of shares had fallen by 90%. The "Bull Market" had been replaced by a "bear market".

The 1920s saw great strides in production techniques, especially in industries like automobiles. The production line allowed for significant economies of scale and great increases in production. However, demand for buying expensive cars and consumer goods were struggling to keep up. Therefore, towards the end of the 1920s many firms were struggling to sell all their production. This caused some of the disappointing profit results that precipitated falls in stock share prices.

In 1929, there were already warning signs from the economy with falling auto sales, lower steel production and a slowdown in housing construction. However, despite these warning signs, people still kept buying shares.

Even before 1929, the American agricultural sector was struggling to maintain profitability. Many small farmers were driven out of business because they could not compete in the new economic climate. Better technology was increasing supply, but demand for food was not increasing at same rate. Therefore, prices fell and the income of farmers dropped. There were occupational and geographical immobility's in this sector, and it was difficult for unemployed farmers to get jobs in other sectors of the economy.

Before the Great Depression, the American banking system was characterized by having many small to medium sized firms. America had over 30,000 banks. The effect of this was that they were prone to going bankrupt if there was a run on deposits. In particular, many banks in rural areas became bankrupt due to the agricultural recession. This had a negative impact on the rest of the financial industry. Between 1923 and 1930 5,000 banks collapsed.

The Great Depression is related to the Wall Street Crash. Modern Economists feel that enough safe guards are in place to avoid a depression in the future. It is said, however, it is a recession when your neighbor has lost his job, but a depression when you have lost yours.

CHAPTER 15

FDR and the New Deal

———

PRESIDENT FRANKLIN ROOSEVELT PROPOSED A series of measures called
The New Deal to combat the effects of the Great Depression. Winning the
nation's presidency in 1932, he advocated for legislation to allow the country
to recover economically and spiritually. His New Deal programs expanded
the size of the federal government, creating a myriad of agencies to put people
to work, rebuild the nations infrastructure, and make improvements in a vari-
ety of areas, including the arts. The goal was to employ people and save the
nation from despair.

One example of a government agency created was the Civil Works
Administration, an entity that expanded and improved America's infrastructure, an expansion that benefited many generations of Americans. Out of a
terrible occurrence, the Great Depression, some good came.

President Roosevelt's New Deal also addresses America's spirit. Elderly
people would no longer live in poverty with the passage of the Social Security
Act, and the implementation of Social Security.

Economists do not agree if the New Deal pulled the USA out of the Great
Depression, but it certainly gave people hope. Critics will say that it expanded
the size of government, which it did. It may also have saved the nation from
anarchy by giving millions a hand up, not a handout.

The New Deal led to a dominance of the Democratic Party, a dominance
that ended in the late 1960's and early 1970's.

CHAPTER 16

The Oil Embargo

———

IN OCTOBER OF 1973 ARAB nations squared off against Israel in what became known as the Yom Kipper War. Egypt and Syria, supported by other Arab nations, attacked Israel. Outnumbered, Israel required and received aid from the United States. Israel was saved, but a stalemate ensued.

Arab nations punished the United States and it's allies by dramatically increasing the price of oil, on which the United States and its allies were heavily dependent.

The Arab action severely impacted not only the economy of the United States, but also the economic climate of the entire world.

The United States, and the rest of the developed world, learned that oil could be used as a weapon, and that dependence on foreign petroleum had serious consequences.

The United States mandated changes in the auto industry to improve gas mileage and somewhat lessen dependence on foreign oil.

This dependence remains today and is a topic of conversation every four years in American presidential campaigns.

CHAPTER 17

The Green Revolution

———

THE WORLD'S POPULATION WAS OUTPACING the capabilities of agriculture to produce enough food for people to survive. For many, an existential crisis was on the horizon. Many nations did not have the agricultural capabilities of feeding their ever-growing populace. Lives were at stake.

Scientists developed new crops and new techniques that allowed for a great increase of agricultural production. Science, agricultural science specifically, saved the day. Nations that previously could not produce enough to meet their own needs often became net exporters of agricultural products.

Higher yields that resulted from scientific breakthroughs not only fed more people, but also lowered the price of basics, benefiting millions worldwide.

There are some downsides to the Green Revolution. Over farming, the use of pesticides and water has caused another set of issues that will need to be dealt with. Shortages of clean water promise to be a major issue in the twenty-first century.

CHAPTER 18

Splitting the Atom: Nuclear Science

———

THE UNITED STATES DEVELOPED AND used the first atomic weapons in 1945 against Japan at the end of World War II. Nuclear power was used in the Soviet Union starting in 1954. Splitting the atom now had practical use.

In 1909 Ernest Rutherford began studying small particles of matter called atoms. In 1917 Rutherford discovered a technique of changing atoms of one element into those of another. He changed nitrogen atoms into oxygen, the first nuclear reaction. This scientific breakthrough led to the first atomic bombs, nuclear reactors, and a very changed world.

CHAPTER 19

The Theory of Relativity

———

IN 1905, ALBERT EINSTEIN PUBLISHED the *theory of special relativity,* which was meant to help us understand the motion between different *inertial frames of reference* — that is, places that are moving at constant speeds relative to each other.

Einstein explained that when two objects are moving at a constant speed as the *relative motion* between the two objects, instead of appealing to the ether as an absolute frame of reference that defined what was going on. If you and another astronaut are moving in different spaceships and want to compare your observations, all that matters is how fast you and that astronaut are moving with respect to each other.

Special relativity includes only the special case (hence the name) where the motion is uniform in nature. The motion it explains is only if you're traveling in a straight line at a constant speed. As soon as you accelerate or curve — or do anything that changes the nature of the motion in any way — special relativity ceases to apply. That's where Einstein's general theory of relativity comes in, because it can explain the general case of any sort of motion.

Einstein's theory is based on two key principles:

- **The principle of relativity:** The laws of physics do not change, even for objects moving in inertial (constant speed) frames of reference.
- **The principle of the speed of light:** The speed of light is the same for all observers, regardless of their motion relative to the light source. (Physicists write this speed using the symbol c.)

The beauty of Einstein's discoveries is that he looked at the experiments and assumed the findings were true. This was the exact opposite of what other physicists seemed to be doing at the time. Instead of assuming the theory was correct and that the experiments failed, he assumed that the experiments were correct and the theory had failed.

In the late 19th century, physicists were searching for the mysterious thing called *ether* — the medium they believed existed for light waves to "wave" through. The belief in ether had caused a mess of things, in Einstein's view, by introducing a medium that caused certain laws of physics to work differently depending on how the observer moved relative to the ether. Einstein just removed the ether entirely and assumed that the laws of physics, including the speed of light, worked the same regardless of how you were moving — exactly as experiments and mathematics showed them to be.

UNIFYING SPACE AND TIME

Einstein's theory of special relativity created an important and fundamental link between space and time. The universe can be viewed as having three space dimensions — up/down, left/right, forward/backward — and one time dimension. This 4-dimensional space is referred to as the *space-time continuum*.

If you move fast enough through space, the observations that you make about space and time differ somewhat from the observations of other people, who are moving at different speeds.

You can imagine this for yourself by understanding a thought experiment. Imagine that you're on a spaceship and holding a laser so it shoots a beam of light directly up, striking a mirror you've placed on the ceiling. The light beam then comes back down and strikes a detector.

However, the spaceship is traveling at a constant speed of half the speed of light ($0.5c$, as physicists would write it). According to Einstein, this makes no difference to you — you can't even tell that you're moving. However, if another astronaut were spying on you it would be a different story.

This astronaut would see your beam of light travel upward along a diagonal path, strike the mirror, and then travel downward along a diagonal path before striking the detector. In other words, you and the other space traveler would see *different* paths for the light and, more importantly, those paths aren't even the same length. This means that the time the beam takes to go from the laser to the mirror to the detector must also be different for you and the other observer so that you both agree on the speed of light.

This phenomenon is known as *time dilation*, where the time on a ship moving very quickly appears to pass slower than on Earth.

As odd as it seems, this example (and many others) demonstrates that in Einstein's theory of relativity, space and time are intimately linked together. If you apply Lorentz transformation equations, they work out so that the speed of light is perfectly consistent for both observers.

This strange behavior of space and time is only evident when you're traveling close to the speed of light, so no one had ever observed it before. Experiments carried out since Einstein's discovery have confirmed that it's true — time and space are perceived differently, in precisely the way Einstein described, for objects moving near the speed of light.

Unifying Mass and Energy

The most famous work of Einstein's life also dates from 1905 when he applied the ideas of his relativity paper to come up with the equation $E=mc2$ that represents the relationship between mass *(m)* and energy *(E)*.

Simply put, Einstein found that as an object approached the speed of light, *c,* the mass of the object increased. The object goes faster, but it also gets heavier. If it were actually able to move at *c,* the object's mass and energy would both be infinite. A heavier object is harder to speed up, so it's impossible to ever actually get the particle up to a speed of *c.*

Until Einstein, the concepts of mass and energy were viewed as completely separate. He proved that the principles of conservation of mass and conservation of energy are part of the same larger, unified principle, *conservation of mass-energy.* Matter can be turned into energy and energy can be turned into matter because a fundamental connection exists between the two types of substance.

Einstein's work has led to the study of Black Holes, nuclear energy, and the scientific embrace of the Big Bang Theory.

CHAPTER 20

The Launch of Sputnik

———

IN 1957 THE SOVIET UNION launched the first in a series of rockets into outer space named Sputnik. The Sputnik program was a major propaganda victory for the Soviet Union at a time of intense competition between Communism and the Free World.

Sputnik not only launched the "Space Race" but also pointed to a perceived Soviet superiority in technology that worried the United States and its western allies.

The Soviet Sputnik program caused the United States to fund and improve scientific research, especially as it related to rocket and space technology.

The United States space program soon outpaced that of the Soviets, and led to a number of innovations and scientific breakthroughs.

More importantly, the travels in space that Sputnik prompted allowed for a sense of optimism and scientific prominence that might otherwise have not occurred.

CHAPTER 21

The Development of the Transistor

———

IN 1956 A SMALL GROUP of research scientists at Bell Labs in the United States conducted research that eventually led to their be awarded the Nobel Prize.

Their task: to develop a device that would improve telephone amplification. Their research led to the development of the transistor. Transistors operate by regulating the amount of electrical current used in a device. It operates as an amplifier; it can take a small electrical current and change it into a more powerful one.

Transistors are very small; they resulted in smaller and more efficient telephones, radios, and other electrical devices.

As radios became less expensive, more portable, and more reliable, more and more people had access to them and the news they provided.

The proliferation of radios, and the information that became more available around the world changed the world.

CHAPTER 22

At the Movies: The Jazz Singer

———

IN 1927 A GREAT INNOVATION in culture occurred. The Jazz Singer, the first "talkie" was released. For the first time, a movie had audible dialog synchronized with the video feed. This movie was so revolutionary, local police were on hand when the film was shown to help quell hysterical and boisterous crowds. It was quite the innovation.

The invention of a process called "the Vitaphone" allowed for the production of movies with synchronized sound.

This breakthrough may have saved Warner Brothers studio.

Movies became a vital and necessary distraction to people during the Great Depression, and powerful force in entertainment, education, and social commentary. Movies could move people, challenge their ideas, and promote worthy (or unworthy) causes.

The Boxer Rebellion

———

PRIOR TO THE TWENTIETH CENTURY China was dominated by foreign powers. Several European nations, Japan, and even the United States maintained spheres of influence within China.

In 1900 the Boxer Rebellion, an indigenous Chinese secret organization called the "Society of the Righteous and Harmonious Fists", began an uprising in the northern portion of China against the spread of Western and Japanese influence there. The rebels, referred to by Westerners, as "Boxers" because they practiced physical exercises they believed would make them able to withstand bullets and other weapons directed against them, killed foreigners and Chinese Christians and destroyed foreign property.

From June to August, the Boxers besieged the foreign district of Beijing (then referred to as Peking), China's capital, until an international force that included many American troops put down the uprising.

By the terms of the Boxer Protocol, which officially ended the rebellion in 1901, China agreed to pay more than $330 million in reparations to the Western powers. A staggering sum in that day.

* The Boxer Rebellion ended with the signing of the Boxer Protocol on September 7, 1901. The terms of the agreement required forts protecting Peking (Beijing) to be destroyed, Boxer and Chinese government officials involved in the uprising were to be sanctioned, foreign

powers were permitted to station troops in Beijing for their defense, and China was prohibited from importing arms for two years.

The lack of success of the Boxer Rebellion delayed the rise of China as a world power, and sewed the seeds of Chinese suspicions of the outside world.

CHAPTER 24

Somme

———

THE BATTLE OF SOMME (JULY 1 to November 13, 1916) was the largest battle in history. Troops from Great Britain and France attempted to retake French territory from German forces. Over one million casualties were suffered.

The immensity of the losses in modern warfare came to light. For the first time, people on all sides questioned the morality of such massive human loses and suffering, especially in a war that seemed destined to be a stalemate.

In the first half day of this battle Great Britain alone suffered 55,000 casualties.

Home front support for this war, and future wars, became uncertain due to the immensity of loss in this battle.

War had lost its luster.

CHAPTER 25

The Failure of the Soviet Union in Afghanistan

———

THE SOVIET UNION INVADED AFGHANISTAN in December of 1979 and stayed for ten years. Their invasion came at the "request" of one of the warring sides in an Afghan civil war. In reality, the Soviet Union was looking to expand its influence, have access to natural resources, and more say in Middle Eastern affairs. Like many things that occurred during the cold war, the Soviet war in Afghanistan became a proxy battle between the United States and the Soviet Union.

Afghan forces fought against the Soviet intervention, and were aided by western powers, including the United States. The United States shipped Afghan fighters anti-aircraft missiles to help negate Soviet air superiority.

The Soviet Union became bogged down against a guerilla insurgency at tremendous cost of blood and treasure. It is thought that the Afghan intervention was "Russia's Vietnam" Many historians felt the Soviets humiliating losses during the Afghan debacle hastened the fall of the Soviet Union.

CHAPTER 26

Apartheid Ends

———

BEGINNING WITH LAWS PASSED IN 1948 South Africa practiced Apartheid (meaning apartness or apart-hood). Apartheid gave legal recognition to different groups: Africans, "Colored", Asians (people of Indian descent), and Chinese. Of course the white European settlers in South Africa had the most rights and the most power. Beginning in 1955, organized resistance to Apartheid began. Resistance and condemnation of Apartheid became a worldwide moral crusade. Apartheid ended in 1994, and Nelson Mandela, a prominent African resident of South Africa and anti-Apartheid activist that had been imprisoned for 27 years eventually became South Africa's president.

The worldwide movement denouncing Apartheid demonstrated the importance of international consensus and the ability of public opinion to right wrongs. Nelson Mandela's rise to power, and willingness to forgive inspired millions around the globe. American Martin Luther King was mentioned by Mandela as an inspiration.

CHAPTER 27

Hiroshima:
The Genie is out of the Bottle

———

AT 8:15 AM IN THE morning on August 6, 1945 the United States used an atomic weapon against Japan, virtually destroying an entire city and killing over 129,000 people. This helped end World War II but gave birth to an era where man could destroy himself. Many are surprised that mankind has survived the 71 years nuclear weapons have existed. At one time, the United States was the only nuclear power. Today Russia, the United Kingdom. France, China, India, Pakistan, Israel, and North Korea all posses "the bomb".

Some geopolitical experts believe nuclear weapons deter war, others feel their existence is an existential danger for mankind.

There is no question that the events of August 6, 1945 changed the course of human history.

President Truman, the American President that ordered the use of the weapon, stated he never lost sleep over the decisions, because many lives on both sides were saved due to the hastened ending of the war. Some perceive Truman as a hero, others as the biggest war criminal in history. This much is certain: It is not fair to judge someone unless you are living in the time of their decision, and living what they had lived.

CHAPTER 28

WWW

———

THE WORLD WIDE WEB BEGAN, as so many things do, because of military or national defense needs. In 1957 DARPA (the Defense Advanced Research Projects Agency) began A "resource sharing" plan connecting research institutions in the United States for use primarily with the space program.

"Arpanet", this resource-sharing plan, eventually became the Internet we know today.

The Internet has changed culture, economies, education, quality of life, and research in unimaginable ways.

What is interesting to note is that funding from the United States Defense Department gave birth to a tool that has changed the world.

CHAPTER 29

HIV

——

HIV (CAUSED BY THE HUMAN Immunodeficiency Virus) is the cause of AIDS, a disease that for some time killed virtually every one of its victims.

HIV can be transmitted in a few different ways, most frequently from sexual contact between an HIV infected person and a sex partner not suffering from the infection.

AIDS is categorized as a zoonosis event. That means AIDS began in the animal kingdom, and jumped species to infect man.

Once a certain death sentence for almost everyone infected, AIDS is now a manageable chronic disease for most that can afford the treatments.

HIV led to tremendous advances in diagnosis, treatment, and prevention of viral and other diseases. Scientific breakthroughs that have resulted from the fight against AIDS are paying dividends to sufferers of many other diseases.

Science and governmental support work well together.

CHAPTER 30

Woodstock

———

RURAL NEW YORK STATE HOSTED the Woodstock music festival from August 15 to August 17, 1969. Over crowded and poorly planned, its legacy to music and the anti-war movement is significant.

The intersection of music, politics, and culture was cemented by the tremendous amount of attention this event received. Attending the festival was an act of defiance against the political status quo, and highlighted the cultural and political influence of musicians and performers.

FRIDAY, AUGUST 15 – SATURDAY, AUGUST 16

Artist	Time	Notes
Richie Havens	5:07 pm – 7:00 pm	
Swami Satchidananda	7:10 pm – 7:20 pm	Gave the opening speech/invocation
Sweetwater	7:30 pm – 8:10 pm	
Bert Sommer	8:20 pm – 9:15 pm	
Tim Hardin	9:20 pm – 9:45 pm	
Ravi Shankar	10:00 pm – 10:35 pm	Played through the rain.
Melanie	10:50 pm – 11:20 pm	
Arlo Guthrie	11:55 pm – 12:25 am	
Joan Baez	12:55 am – 2:00 am	Was six months pregnant.

SUNDAY, AUGUST 17 – MONDAY, AUGUST 18

Artist	Time	Notes
Joe Cocker and The Grease Band	2:00 pm – 3:25 pm	Played "With A Little Help From My Friends." After Joe Cocker's set, a thunderstorm disrupted the events for several hours.
Country Joe and the Fish	6:30 pm – 8:00 pm	Country Joe McDonald's second performance.
Ten Years After	8:15 pm – 9:15 pm	
The Band	10:00 pm – 10:50 pm	
Johnny Winter	12:00 am – 1:05 am	Winter's brother, Edgar Winter, is featured on three songs.
Blood, Sweat & Tears	1:30 am – 2:30 am	
Crosby, Stills, Nash & Young	3:00 am – 4:00 am	An acoustic and electric set were played. Neil Young skipped most of the acoustic set.
Paul Butterfield Blues Band	6:00 am – 6:45 am	
Sha Na Na	7:30 am – 8:00 am	
Jimi Hendrix / Gypsy Sun & Rainbows	9:00 am – 11:10 am	Performed to a considerably smaller crowd of fewer than 200,000 people.

Artist	Time	Notes
Quill	12:15 pm – 12:45 pm	
Country Joe McDonald	1:00 pm – 1:30 pm	Joe later performed together with The Fish.
Santana	2:00 pm – 2:45 pm	Michael Shrieve, the band's drummer, was the youngest musician to play at the festival.
John Sebastian	3:30 pm – 3:55 pm	Sebastian was not on the bill, but rather was attending the festival, and was recruited to perform while the promoters waited for many of the scheduled performers to arrive.
Keef Hartley Band	4:45 pm – 5:30 pm	
The Incredible String Band	6:00 pm – 6:30 pm	
Canned Heat	7:30 pm – 8:30 pm	
Mountain	9:00 pm – 10:00 pm	This performance was only their third gig as a band.
Grateful Dead	10:30 pm – 12:05 am	Their set was cut short after the stage amps overloaded during "Turn On Your Love Light".
Creedence Clearwater Revival	12:30 am – 1:20 am	
Janis Joplin with The Kozmic Blues Band[37]	2:00 am – 3:00 am	
Sly and the Family Stone	3:30 am – 4:20 am	
The Who	5:00 am – 6:05 am	Briefly interrupted by Abbie Hoffman.
Jefferson Airplane	8:00 am – 9:40 am	Joined onstage by former Jeff Beck Group piano player Nicky Hopkins.

TIMELINE OF THE TWENTIETH CENTURY IN NORTH AMERICA:

1900:   The first mass-market camera, the "Brownie" is introduced by Kodak

1900:   Approximately 2,300 automobiles are registered in the U.S.

1900:   Only 5% of USA households own a telephone

1900:   Life expectancy in the US is 47.3

1901:   One million people emigrate from Europe to the US in just a year

1901:   16,000 patents are filed in just one year

1902:   Irrigation of the western lands begins

1902:   USA architect Daniel Burnham designs the "Flatiron" in New York

1903:   Wilbur and Orville Wright fly the first airplane

1903:   Edwin Porter directs the film "The Great Train Robbery"

1904:   The USA writer Henry James publishes the novel "The Golden Bowl"

1904:   Harvey Hubbell invents the electrical plug and socket

1905:   Expressionism is born in Dresden with the group "Die Bruecke"

1905:   The comic strip "Little Nemo" by Winsor Mccay debuts

1906:   Lee deForrest invents the vacuum tube

1906:   The San Francisco earthquake and fire

1907:   Leo Baekeland invents the first plastic ("bakelite")

1907:   Florenz Ziegfeld's "Ziegfeld Follies" debut

1908:   Ford introduces the Model T, the first mass vehicle

1908:   William D'Arcy discovers oil in Iran

1908:   Durant founds General Motors in Detroit

1909:   The average hourly salary in the USA is $0.19

1909:   The Metlife tower in Madison Square is the tallest building in the world

1909:   Stanford University's president David Starr Jordan invests $500 in Lee deForrest's audion tube, the first major venture-capital investment in the region

1909:   Charles Herrold in San Jose starts the first radio station in the USA with regularly scheduled programming

1909:   Cyril Elwell founds the Federal Telegraph Corporation (FTC) in Palo Alto to create the world's first global radio communication system

1910: The NAACP is founded to protect the rights of African Americans

1910: Los Angeles opens the first international airport in the USA

1910: California produces 22% of the world's oil (more than any country in the world)

1910: The first Nickelodeon (movie theater) theater opens in Los Angeles

1910: David-Ward Griffith directs the film "Old California" in the little village of Hollywood, north of Los Angeles

1911: General Electric introduces the first commercial refrigerator

1911: Hollerith's Tabulating Machine Company is acquired by a new company that will change name to International Bussiness Machines or IBM in 1924

1912: Mack Sennett founds the "Keystone Studios" to produce "slapstick" films

1913: John Rockefeller is worth $212 billions, 1/44th of the USA economy

1913: The "Ziegfeld Follies" launch the first "dance crazy", the "foxtrot"

1913: Ford installs the first assembly line (at Highland Park)

1913: USA architect Cass Gilbert designs the Woolworth Building in New York

1914: Marcus Garvey founds the "Universal Negro Improvement Association"

1914: The USA and Panama open the Panama Canal

1915: The USA has 100 million people, of which 13-15% are foreign-born

1915: The majority of USA films are made in the Los Angeles area

1915: William Simmons founds the racist "Ku Klux Klan"

1915: The Panama-Pacific International Exposition is held in San Francisco, for which Bernard Maybeck builds the Palace of Fine Arts in San Francisco

1915: David-Ward Griffith directs the film "The Birth of a Nation"

1916: Charles Ives composes his "Symphony 4"

1916: William Boeing founds a company to manufacture airplanes

1917: Edwin Pridham and Peter Jensen found the electronics company Magnavox in Napa

1917: Columbia University establishes the Pulitzer Prize

1917: 40% of USA households own a telephone

1917:   The Original Dixieland Jass Band makes the first recording of "dix-
        ieland jazz"

1917:   The USA accounts for 67% of the world's oil output

1917:   The USA enters World War I

1918:   An epidemics of influenza kills 20 million people worldwide (500,000
        in the USA)

1919:   The USA overtakes Europe as total industrial output

1919:   Barnum and Bailey's circus merges with the Ringling Brothers to
        form the "Ringling Brothers and Barnum and Bailey Circus"

1920:   Universal female suffrage in the USA

1920:   Mamie Smith makes the first blues recording

1921:   The first fax is sent by Western Union

1921:   Ansel Adams publishes his first photographs of Yosemite

1922:   There are 60,000 radios in the USA

1923:   The "Cotton Club" opens in Harlem, featuring only black entertain-
        ers but catering to a white-only audience

1923:   James Johnson's musical "Runnin' Wild" launches the dance craze of
        the "charleston"

1925:   Frederick Terman joins Stanford University to teach electronics elec-
        trical engineering and encourages his students to start businesses in
        California

1925:   The "Revue Negre" in Paris introduces African-American entertainer
        Josephine Baker dancing the "charleston"

1925:   Burroughs introduces a portable adding machine

1925:   Louis Armstrong forms the Hot Five in Chicago

1925:   The USA writer Francis-Scott Fitzgerald publishes the novel "The
        Great Gatsby"

1925:   George Antheil composes the "Ballet Mecanique"

1926:   Films with synchronized voice and music are introduced

1926:   Alexander Calder creates the kinetic sculpture "Cirque Calder"

1927:   Philo Farnsworth invents the television in San Francisco

1927:   Jerome Kern and Oscar Hammerstein create the musical "Show Boat"

1927:   The first talking movie is "The Jazz Singer"

1927: Lindberg flies from New York to Paris

1929: 78% of the world's cars are in the USA

1929: There are 10 million radios in the USA

1929: Stock markets crash around the world and beginning of the "Great Depression"

1929: The Museum of Modern Art is founded in New York

1929: The comic strip "Popeye" by Elzie Crisler Segar debuts

1929: The comic strip "Buck Rogers" by Phil Nowlan & Dick Calkins debuts

1930: The comic strip "Mickey Mouse" by 1930, Walt Disney & Ub Iwerks debuts

1930: The USA poet Hart Crane writes "The Bridge"

1930: USA architect William van Alen designs the Chrysler Building in New York

1931: The comic strip "Dick Tracy" by 1931, Chester Gould debuts

1931: The Empire State Building, the tallest building in the world of all times, opens in New York

1931: Duke Ellington's "Creole Rhapsody" takes both sides of a 7" record

1931: Ernest Lawrence designs the first successful cyclotron and founds the Lawrence Berkeley Laboratories

1932: The USA writer William Faulkner publishes the novel "Light in August"

1932: A Duke Ellington hit features the word "swing" in the title

1933: The Marx Brothers make the film "Duck Soup"

1933: President Franklin Roosevelt launches the "New Deal"

1933: The experimental university Black Mountain College is founded in North Carolina with an interdisciplinary approach

1933: The comic strip "Brick Bradford" by 1933, Clarence Gray & William Ritt debuts

1933: The Navy opens a base at NAS Sunnyvale (later renamed Moffett Field)

1934: The "Apollo" night-club opens in Harlem

1934: George-Herbert Mead publishes "Mind, Self and Society"

1934: The comic strip "Flash Gordon" by Alex Raymond debuts

1934: The comic strip "Li'l Abner" by Al Capp debuts

1934: The comic strip "Secret Agent X-9" by Dashiell Hammett & Alex Raymond debuts

1935: Wallace Carothers invents nylon, the first totaly synthetic fibre

1935: A concert by the Benny Goodman's jazz orchestra is broadcast live

1935: George Gershwin composes the folk opera "Porgy And Bess", influenced by black music

1935: The Eastman Kodak Company introduces the "Kodachrome", the first color film

1936: Georgia O'Keeffe paints "Summer Days"

1936: Charles Chaplin directs the film "Modern Times"

1936: Martha Graham choreographes the ballet "Chronicle"

1936: San Francisco builds the longest bridge in the world, the "Bay Bridge"

1936: Alan Turing describes a machine capable of performing logical reasoning, the "Turing Machine"

1936: John Lawrence, brother of Lawrence Berkeley Labs' founder, starts the Donner Laboratory to conduct research in nuclear medicine

1937: Fred Terman's students William Hewlett and David Packard start a company to produce their audio-oscillator

1937: Stanford University's professor William Hansen teams with brothers Sigurd and Russell Varian to develop the klystron tube, used in the early radars

1937: The Golden Gate Bridge is completed in San Francisco

1937: Chester Carlson invents the photocopier

1938: Charles Morris publishes "Foundations of the Theory of Signs"

1938: Howard Hawks directs the film "Bringing Up Baby"

1938: The comic strip "Superman" by Jerome Siegel and Joe Shuster debuts

1938: The comic strip "Mandrake" by Lee Falk and Phil Davis debuts

1938: John Atanasoff at at Iowa State College conceives the electronic digital computer

1939: Walt Disney becomes the first customer of Hewlett-Packard, purchasing their oscillator for the animation film "Fantasia"

1939: Ernest Lawrence is awarded the Nobel Prize in Physics

1939: The USA government establishes the Ames Aeronautical Laboratory (later renamed Ames Research Center) at Moffett Field

1939: John Ford directs the film "Stagecoach"

1939: Pan American inaugurates the world's first transatlantic passenger service, flying between New York and Marseilles

1939: John Cage composes "Imaginary Landscape N.1" for magnetic tape

1939: The comic strip "Batman" by Bill Finger and Bob Kane debuts

1940: The first freeway is built in Los Angeles

1940: The comic strip "Spirit" by Will Eisner debuts

1940: Peter Goldmark invents color television

1940: Friz Freleng's cartoon "You Ought to Be in Pictures" combines live action and animation

1940: John Von Neumann makes a distinction between data and instructions

1941: Stanford University's professor Fred Terman is put in charge of the top-secret Harvard Radio Research Laboratory

1941: First casino opens on on what would become the Las Vegas Strip

1941: Glenn Seaborg and Edwin McMillan at UC Berkeley produce a new element, plutonium

1941: Walker Evans publishes the photograph series "Let Us Now Praise Famous Men"

1941: Orson Welles directs the film "Citizen Kane"

1941: Japan attacks Pearl Harbor (Hawaii) and the USA enters World War II

1941: Dizzy Gillespie, Charlie Parker, Thelonious Monk and Kenny Clarke jam in a new jazz style, "bebop"

1942: Enrico Fermi achieves the first nuclear reaction in Chicago

1942: The USA poet Wallace Stevens writes "Notes Towards A Supreme Fiction"

1942: The USA government launches the "Manhattan Project" to build a nuclear bomb under the direction of Robert Oppenheimer, a professor of Physics at UC Berkeley

1943: Tommy Flowers and others build the Colossus, the world's first programmable digital electronic computer

1943: Warren McCulloch and Walter Pitts describe an artificial neuron

1943: The first "New York Fashion Week" or "Press Week" is held in New York, the world's first fashion show

1944: Everette DeGolyer announces that the Arabian peninsula, Iraq and Iran hold colossal reserves of oil

1944: Richard Rodgers and Oscar Hammerstein create the musical "Oklahoma", choreographed by Agnes de Mille

1944: The world's monetary system is anchored to the dollar and the dollar to gold ("Bretton Woods agreement")

1944: Frank Malina founds the Jet Propulsion Laboratory (JPL)

1944: Howard Aiken of IBM unveils the first computer programmed by punched paper tape, the Harvard Mark I

1945: Germany surrenders and is divided in a Western and a Soviet area, while Soviet troops occupy Eastern European countries

1945: The USA drops two atomic bombs on Japan (Hiroshima and Nagasaki) and World War II ends

1945: The United Nations Organization is founded in New York

1945: Earl Tupper founds Tupperware to make polyethylene plastic containers for home use

1945: Jackson Pollock begins experimenting a "drip" technique of painting that heralds the age of Abstract Expressionism

1945: Wiliam de Kooning paints "Pink Angels"

1945: Mark Rothko paints "Slow Swirl at Edge of Sea"

1945: Vannevar Bush proposes the "Memex" desk-based machine

1946: Frank Capra directs the film "It's A Wonderful Life"

1946: The first venture capital firms are founded in the USA, American Research and Development Corporation (ARDC) by former Harvard Business School's dean Georges Doriot, J.H. Whitney & Company by John Hay Whitney, Rockefeller Brothers by Laurance Rockefeller (later renamed Venrock)

1946: The first two venture capital firms are founded in the USA, American Research and Development Corporation (ARDC) and J.H. Whitney & Company.

1946: Churchill delivers in the USA the "Iron Curtain" speech, virtually opening the "Cold War" against the Soviet Union

1946:   George Marshall envisions a plan to promote the economic recovery of European democracies

1946:   RCA Victor releases the first vinyl record

1946:   TWA and United begin transcontinental flights from New York to California

1946:   The Stanford Research Institute is founded

1946:   John Northrop and Wendell Stanley of UC Berkeley are awarded the Nobel Prize in Chemistry

1946:   Fred Terman returns to Stanford University as the dean of the engineering school and founds the Electronics Research Lab (ERL), mostly founded by the USA military

1946:   The first non-military computer, ENIAC, or "Electronic Numerical Integrator and Computer", is unveiled, built by John Mauchly and Presper Eckert of the Sperry-Rand Corporation

1947:   AT&T Bell Telephone Laboratory's engineers John Bardeen, William Shockley and Walter Brattain demonstrate the principle of amplifying an electrical current using a solid semiconducting material, i.e. the "transistor"

1947:   Norbert Wiener founds Cybernetics

1947:   John Von Neumann describes a self-reproducing automata

1947:   The first widely publicized sighting of a UFO

1947:   Edwin Land invents Polaroid, the first instant camera

1947:   The USA sets up the Central Intelligence Agency (CIA)

1947:   The USA playwright Tennessee Williams stages "A Streetcar Named Desire"

1948:   The Varian brothers found Varian Associates

1948:   The "American Society of Human Genetics" (ASHG) is established

1948:   Claude Shannon founds Information Theory and coins the term "bit"

1949:   William Giauque of UC Berkeley is awarded the Nobel Prize in Chemistry)

1948:   Invention of "xerography" (copying machines) by Chester Carlson

1948:   Senator Joseph McCarthy launches a "witch hunt" against intellectuals suspected of being communist

1949:   NATO is formed by western European countries and USA

1949:   The USA playwright Arthur Miller stages "Death of a Salesman"

1949:   Miles Davis' nonet inaugurates "cool jazz"

1949:   The first foreign car, the Volkswagen Beetle, is sold in the USA, which is also the first "compact" ever sold in the USA

1949:   John Parsons designs the first numerical-control system for machine tools

1949:   The USA government funds the project for a "Semi Automatic Ground Environment" (SAGE) for enemy bomber detection, mainly developed by IBM ("Project AN/FSQ-7") and the MIT ("Project Whirlwind")

1950:   United Nations troops led by the USA push back Chinese troops in Korea

1950:   The comic strip "Charlie Brown" by Charles Schulz debuts

1950:   Billy Wilder directs the film "Sunset Boulevard"

1950:   Turing proposes a test to determine whether a machine is intelligent or not

1950:   Remington purchases Eckert-Mauchly Computer

1951:   The Stanford Industrial Park is conceived

1951:   Charles Ginsburg of Ampex Corporation builds the first practical videotape recorder

1951:   Glenn Seaborg and Edwin McMillan are awarded the Nobel Prize

1951:   The first commercial computer is built, the Univac

1951:   A team led by Jay Forrester at the MIT builds the "Whirlwind" computer, the first real-time system and the first computer to use a video display for output

1951:   John Huston directs the film "The African Queen"

1951:   William Boyle invents the credit card

1951:   USA architect Philip Johnson designs the Lever House in New York

1951:   The first rock and roll record, Ike Turner's "Rocket 88", is released

1951:   Carl Djerassi invents synthetic progesterone, "the birth-control pill", at Syntex of Mexico City

1952:   73% of world cars are produced in the USA

1952:   Art critic Harold Rosenberg coins the term "action painting"

1952: A concert of electronic music by Otto Luening and Vladimir Ussachevsky at New York's Museum Of Modern Art is broadcasted live

1952: IBM opens its first West Coast laboratory in San Jose

1952: Felix Bloch of Stanford University is awarded the Nobel Prize in Physics

1952: The Atomic Energy Commission establishes a Livermore Laboratory as a branch of the UC Berkeley's Radiation Laboratory

1953: Varian is the first tenant of the Stanford Industrial Park

1953: Electronics manufacturer Sylvania opens its Electronic Defense Lab (EDL) in Mountain View

1953: Lawrence Ferlinghetti founds a bookstore in San Francisco, "City Lights", that becomes the headquarters of alternative writers

1953: Remington Rand introduces UNIVAC 1103, the first computer with Random Access Memory or "RAM"

1953: Merce Cunningham at the Black Mountain Collegeforms the Merce Cunningham Dance Company, that uses chance operations to choreograph ballets and set designs by painter Robert Rauschenberg

1953: The USA and Britain engineer a coup to remove Iran's prime minister Mohammad Mossadegh

1953: The USA playwright Eugene O'Neill stages "Long Day's Journey"

1953: Francis Crick and James Watson discover the double helix of the DNA

1954: The first commercial transistor radio, the Regency TR-1, is introduced by IDEA, using circuits by Texas Instruments

1954: Art Blakey and Horace Silver form the Jazz Messengers and coin "hard bop"

1954: Elia Kazan directs the film "On the Waterfront"

1955: The first conference on Artificial Intelligence is held at Dartmouth College, organized by John McCarthy

1955: Allen Ginsberg's recitation of his poem "Howl" transplants the "Beat" aesthetic to San Francisco

1955: Private investors or "angels" (including John Bryan, Bill Edwards and Reid Dennis) establish "The Group" to invest together in promising companies

1955:   Alexander Schure founds the New York Institute of Technology

1955:   Remington Rand merges with Sperry to form Sperry Rand

1955:   Stanford University merges the Applied Electronics Laboratory and the Electronics Research Laboratory into the Systems Engineering Laboratory under the direction of Fred Terman and focusing on electronic warfare

1955:   Harry Olson and Herbert Belar at RCA's Princeton Labs unveil the first "electronic music synthesizer"

1955:   Rock and roll records climb the charts

1955:   The first McDonald's restaurant opens near Chicago

1955:   Chuck Berry cuts his first rock and roll records, the first ones to have the guitar as the main instrument

1955:   Ray Charles invents "soul" music

1955:   Disneyland opens in Los Angeles

1955:   The USA writer William Gaddis publishes the novel "The Recognitions"

1955:   The first numerical-control machine tool, controlled by the "Numericord NC5", is deployed by the Giddings and Lewis Machine Tool Company

1955:   Martin Luther King organizes non-violent protests against racial segregation

1956:   USA architect Frank Lloyd Wright designs the Guggenheim Museum in New York

1956:   Don Siegel directs the film "Invasion of the Body Snatchers"

1956:   William Shockley founds the Shockley Transistor Corporation in Mountain View to produce semiconductor-based transistors to replace vacuum tubes, and hires Robert Noyce, Gordon Moore and others

1956:   Aircraft company Lockheed opens an electronics research laboratory in the Stanford Industrial Park and a manufacturing facility in Sunnyvale

1956:   Werner Buchholz of IBM coins the term "byte"

1957:   Several engineers (including Robert Noyce and Gordon Moore) quit the Shockley Transistor laboratories and form Fairchild Semiconductor in Mountain View, using funding from Fairchild Camera and

Instrument, to mass-produce "integrated circuits" (micro-sized silicon devices containing a large number of electronic switches)

1957: Former SAGE engineer Ken Olsen founds the Digital Equipment Corporation

1957: Max Mathews begins composing computer music at Bell Laboratories

1957: Dean Watkins of Stanford's ERL founds Watkins-Johnson, one of the first venture-capital funded companies in the Santa Clara Valley

1957: Allen Newell and Herbert Simon develop the "General Problem Solver"

1957: Frank Rosenblatt conceives the "Perceptron", a neural computer that can learn by trial and error

1957: Morton Heilig invents the "Sensorama Machine", a pioneering virtual-reality environment

1957: Jean-Paul Getty is the richest man in the USA and its only billionaire

1957: Albert Sabin develops the polio vaccine

1957: 4.5 million babies are born in the USA, the highest number in its history (the "baby boomers")

1957: A computer composes the Illiac Suite, using software created by Lejaren Hiller

1957: LaMonte Young composes music for sustained tones

1957: Noam Chomsky speculates that humans have an innate universal grammar that is a based on logical rules

1958: IBM starts production of the AN/FSQ-7 computer, the largest computer ever built, for the SAGE project

1958: Robert Frank publishes the photograph series "The Americans"

1958: The USA poet William-Carlos Williams writes "Paterson"

1958: The USA's gross national product is 50% of the world's national product

1958: The USA government sets up the National Aeronautics and Space Agency (NASA) as well as the the Defense Advanced Research Projects Agency (DARPA)

1958: John Kenneth Galbraith publishes "The Affluent Society"

1958: Robert Noyce (at Fairchild) and Jack Kilby (at Texas Instruments) invent the integrated circuit

1958: Charles Townes of Columbia theorizes about an optical maser and his student Gordon Gould builds one and names it "LASER" or "Light Amplification by the Stimulated Emission of Radiation"

1958: Draper, Gaither and Anderson is founded, the first venture-capital firm in California

1958: Jim Backus of IBM invents the FORTRAN programming language, the first machine-independent language

1958: NASA opens a research center near Mountain View

1959: War erupts between Soviet-sponsored regime of North Vietnam, led by Ho Chi Minh, and the USA-sponsored regime of South Vietnam

1959: The MIT launches the "Computer-Aided Design Project"

1959: The first commercial Xerox machine goes on sale

1959: Dancer and mime Ron Davis founds the San Francisco Mime Troupe as an experimental project of the now-legendary Actors' Workshop

1959: Arthur Kornberg of Stanford University is awarded the Nobel Prize in Medicine

1959: Emilio Segre and Owen Chamberlain of the Lawrence Berkeley Labs are awarded the Nobel Prize for the discovery of the antiproton

1959: Frank Chambers founds the venture-capital company Continental Capital

1959: GTE buys Sylvania

1959: Mattel introduces the doll "Barbie"

1959: Allan Kaprow launches the vogue of "happenings" (performance art) with "18 Happenings in 6 Parts"

1959: Ornette Coleman's "The Shape of Jazz to Come" debuts free-jazz

1959: John Cage performs "live electronic music"

1959: Lithuanian-born artist George Maciunas organizes the "Fluxus" art movement in New York, inspired by Dada

1959: USA writer William Burroughs and British painter Brion Gysin develop the "cut-up" technique

1959: Alfred Hitchcock directs the film "North By Northwest"

1959: The first numerical-control machine controlled by "Automatically Programmed Tool" or APT, a programming language for numerical control, is demonstrated by the MIT

1950: Akira Kurosawa directs the film "Rashomon"
1950: The Italian writer Cesare Pavese publishes the novel "The Moon and the Bonfire"
1950: The Chilean poet Pablo Neruda writes "Canto General"
1950: Germany's GDP between 1950 and 1955 grows at an average annual rate of 9.1% (the "Economic Miracle")
1951: Karlheinz Stockhausen begins composing "electronic music"
1951: David Bohm hypothesizes that Quantum Mechanics requires a fifth dimension
1951: Andre Bazin founds the film magazine "Cahiers du Cinema"
1951: The cinema magazine "Cahiers du Cinema" is founded by critic Andre Bazin
1952: French architect LeCorbusier designs the Chandigarh High Court in India
1952: The German poet Paul Celan writes "Poppy and Memory"
1952: The British poet David Jones writes "The Anathemata"
1952: The Irish playwright Samuel Beckett stages "Waiting for Godot"
1952: Japanese companies license the technology of the transistor from the USA
1952: The Mau Mau guerrillas pledge to drive white people out of Kenya
1952: Gamal Nasser abolishes the monarchy and seizes power in Egypt
1952: Peron's wife Eva dies of cancer in Argentina as millions mourn her as a saint
1953: Lev Rudnev designs the Lomonosov University in Moscow
1953: The Cuban writer Alejo Carpentier publishes the novel "The Lost Steps"
1954: The "Front de Liberation Nationale" (FLN) of Algeria begins an independence war against France
1954: European countries found CERN, the "Centre Europeen pour la Recherche Nucleaire"
1954: Benjamin Britten composes the opera "Turn Of The Screw"
1954: Iannis Xenakis composes "Metastasis", with independent parts for every musician of the orchestra
1954: Pierre Boulez composes "Le Marteau Sans Maitre"

1954: Jiro Yoshihara founds the "Gutai Group" in Japan that pioneers performance art

1955: Arnold Bode founds the "Documenta" exhibition of art in Germany

1955: The Spanish writer Rafael Sanchez-Ferlosio publishes the novel "The River El Jarama"

1956: The Italian poet Eugenio Montale writes "The Storm"

1956: The Hungarian poet Sandor Weores writes "The Tower of Silence"

1956: The Czech poet Vladimir Holan writes "A Night with Hamlet"

1956: Egyptian president Gamal Abdel Nasser of Egypt nationalizes the Suez Canal

1956: The Swiss playwright Friedrich Duerrenmatt stages "The Visit"

1956: Atsuko Tanaka's "Electric Dress" pioneers performance-art

1956: Luigi Nono composes "Canto Sospeso"

1956: Brazilian president Juscelino Kubitschek founds a new capital, Brasilia

1956: An anti-communist uprising led by Imre Nagy in Hungary is crushed by Soviet troops

1956: The first world congress of Human Genetics is held in Copenhagen

1957: Ghana becomes the first black African country to win independence from a European power

1957: The Soviet Union launches the Sputnik, the first artificial satellite

1957: Bruno Maderna's "Musica su Due Dimensioni" is the first "electro-acoustic" composition, mixing traditional instruments and electronic tape

1957: Italy, Germany, France and others found the European Economic Community

1957: Ingmar Bergman directs the film "Wild Strawberries"

1957: The Italian writer Elsa Morante publishes the novel "Arthur's Island"

1957: The Australian writer Patrick White publishes the novel "Voss"

1957: German architect Ludwig Mies van der Rohe builds the Seagram Building in New York

1957: The Italian poet Pierpaolo Pasolini writes "The Ashes of Gramsci"

1957: Asger Jorn and Guy Debord lead the "Situationist International" in Italy, an international group of intellectuals and artists inspired by Marxism and Surrealism

1958: The Swiss playwright Max Frisch stages "Biedermann"

1958: Brazilian architect Oscar Niemeyer designs the Congress Complex in Brasilia

1958: Claude Chabrol's film "Le Beau Serge" inaugurates the "Nouvelle Vague" of French cinema

1958: Wolf Vostell creates the first "Decollage" happening in Paris

1959: Tatsumi Hijikata's "Forbidden Colours" invents "butoh" dance

1959: The Dalai Lama of Tibet flees to India

1959: The British Motor Corporation introduces the "Mini"

1959: 38 million Chinese starve to death because of the 1959-62 famine caused by Mao's "Great Leap Forward"

1959: Fidel Castro leads a communist revolution in Cuba

1959: The comic strip "Asterix" by Rene' Goscinny and Albert Uderzo debuts

1959: The Paraguayan writer Augusto Roa-Bastos publishes the novel "Son of Man"

1959: The French writer Raymond Queneau publishes the novel "Zazie in the Metro"

1959: Louis Kahn designs the Salk Institute in La Jolla

1959: Giacinto Scelsi composes "Quattro Pezzi per Una Nota Sola", micro-music for only one note

1959: The French playwright Eugene Ionesco stages "Rhinoceros"

1959: The British playwright John Arden stages "Serjeant Musgrave's Dance"

1959: The Greek poet Odysseus Elytis writes "Worthy It Is"

1960: Jean Tinguely creates a kinetic sculpture, "Homage to New York", that destroys itself

1960: John Whitney pioneers computer animation

1960: William Fetter of Boeing coins the expression "computer graphics"

1960: Theodore Maiman of the Hughes Research Laboratory demonstrates the first working laser

1960: Donald Glaser of the Lawrence Berkeley Labs is awarded the Nobel Prize

1961:   Roy Lichtenstein paints "Look Mickey"

1961:   Roger Reynolds, Robert Ashley and Gordon Mumma organize the first "ONCE" festival of avantgarde music at Ann Arbor in Michigan

1961:   James Tenney composes the computer music of "Noise Study"

1961:   Lou Harrison composes "Concerto in Slendro"

1961:   Charles Bachman at General Electric develops the first database management system, IDS

1961:   Philco unveils the first head-mounted display

1961:   IBM owns more than 81% of the computer market

1961:   General Motors unveils "Unimate", the first industrial robot

1961:   Robert Hofstadter of Stanford University is awarded the Nobel Prize in Physics

1961:   Melvin Calvin of the Lawrence Berkeley Labs is awarded the Nobel Prize

1961:   Tommy Davis founds one of Santa Clara Valley's first venture-capital firms with Arthur Rock, Davis & Rock

1962:   The San Francisco Tape Music Center for avantgarde music is established by composers Morton Subotnick and and Ramon Sender

1962:   Helen Gurley Brown publishes "Sex and the Single Girl"

1962:   Andy Warhol exhibits his pop-art work "Marilyn Diptych"

1962:   The USA lifts into orbit the first telecommunication satellite, the Telstar

1962:   Helen Gurley Brown publishes "Sex and the single girl"

1962:   The comic book "Spiderman" by Stan Lee debuts

1962:   Itek introduces the first commercial CAD system, "Electronic Drafting Machine", built by former SAGE engineers

1962:   Paul Baran proposes a distributed network as the form of communication least vulnerable to a nuclear strike

1962:   Stanford University founds the Stanford Linear Accelerator Center

1963:   Douglas Engelbart at the Stanford Research Institute builds the first prototype of the "mouse"

1963:   Edward Zajac of Bell Labs creates a computer-generated film

1963:   The "American Standard Code for Information Interchange" or "ASCII" is introduced

1968: Stewart Brand publishes the first "Whole Earth Catalog"

1963: Ivan Sutherland of the MIT demonstrates "Sketchpad", a computer graphics program, and the first program ever with a graphical user interface

1963: President John Kennedy is assassinated

1963: Bob Dylan releases "Blowin' In The Wind"

1963: Bell Labs introduces the touch-tone phone

1963: Lukas Foss composes "Echoi", that employs improvisation

1963: Buddhist monk Thich Quang Duc sets himself on fire in a busy street of South Vietnam's capital

1964: Milton Babbitt composes "Ensembles For Synthesizer"

1964: Syntex introduces the birth-control pill

1964: The USA writer Saul Bellow publishes the novel "Herzog"

1964: Engineer Michael Callahan, painter Stephen Durkee and poet Gerd Stern found USCO ("The Company of Us"), a multimedia art collective that employs electronic devices

1964: Charles Csuri creates the first computer art

1964: IBM introduces the first "mainframe" computer, the 360, and the first "operating system", the OS/360

1964: Robert Moog begins selling his synthesizer

1964: Mario Savio founds the "Free Speech Movement" and leads student riots at the Berkeley campus

1964: Ken Kesey organizes the "Merry Pranksters" who travel around the country in a "Magic Bus", live in a commune in La Honda and experiment with "acid tests" (LSD)

1964: John Kemeny and Thomas Kurtz (at Dartmouth College invent the BASIC programming language)

1964: American Airlines' SABRE reservation system, developed by IBM, is the first online transaction processing

1964: Former Sylviania employee Bill Perry founds computer-based electronic-intelligence company ESL

1964: The "Tonkin Gulf Incident", presented by the USA as an attack on its warships, triggers a massive escalation of USA intervention in Vietnam

1965: Gordon Moore predicts that the processing power of computers will double every 18 months

1965: Former Ampex employee Ray Dolby founds the Dolby Labs while in Britain (relocating it to San Francisco in 1976)

1965: Ron Davis of the San Francisco Mime Troupe publishes the essay "Guerrilla Theatre"

1965: The Family Dog Production organizes the first hippie festival in San Francisco

1965: Terry Riley composes "In C", music based on repetition of simple patterns ("minimalism")

1965: Edward Feigenbaum leads development of the expert system "Dendral" at Stanford University

1965: George Hunter of the Charlatans introduces the "light show" in rock concerts

1965: The Digital Equipment Corporation unveils the first mini-computer, the PDP-8, that uses integrated circuits

1965: Alan Hovhaness composes "Fantasy on Japanese Woodprints"

1965: Robert Aldrich directs the film "Hush Hush Sweet Charlotte"

1966: Frederic Rzewski, Alvin Curran and Richard Teitelbaum form the ensemble of live electronic music Musica Elettronica Viva in Rome

1966: The USA writer John Barth publishes the novel "Giles Goat Boy"

1966: Fluxus member Dick Higgins coins the term "Intermedia" to describe art that straddles multiple genres

1966: The first "Summer of Love" of the hippies is held in San Francisco

1966: Hewlett-Packard enters the business of general-purpose computers with the HP-2115

1966: Willie Brown organizes the Artists Liberation Front of San Francisco-based artists at the Mime Troupe's Howard Street loft

1966: The first issue of the San Francisco Oracle, an underground cooperative publication, is published

1966: Emmett Grogan and members of the Mime Troupe found the "Diggers", a group of improvising actors and activists whose stage was the streets and parks of the Haight-Ashbury and whose utopia was the creation of a Free City

1966:   Huey Newton, Bobby Seale, Angela Davis and other African-American activists found the socialist-inspired and black-nationalist "Black Panther Party" at Oakland

1966:   There are 2,623 computers in the USA (1,967 work for the Defense Department)

1966:   Donald Buchla develops a voltage-controlled synthesizer for composer Morton Subotnick, the Buchla Modular Electronic Music System

1966:   The Asian Art Museum of San Francisco is inaugurated

1967:   Jack Kilby (at Texas Instruments develops the first hand-held calculator)

1967:   Ray Browne founds the "Center for the Study of Popular Culture" at Bowling Green, that popularizes the term "pop culture"

1967:   Darryl McCray, or "Cornbread", creates graffiti art in Philadelphia

1967:   A "Human Be-In" is held at the Golden Gate Park in San Francisco

1967:   Monterey hosts a rock festival

1967:   Nam June Paik pioneers video art with his "Participation TV", an interactive video installation

1967:   Frank Stella paints "Harran II"

1967:   The USA has 200 million people, of which 9.7 million are foreign-born

1967:   USA architect Buckminster Fuller designs a geodesic dome for the USA Pavillion at the Expo in Montreal

1967:   Bands such as the Velvet Underground, the Doors and Pink Floyd launch psychedelic-rock

1968:   Harold Morowitz publishes "Energy FLow in Biology"

1968:   Roman Polanski directs the film "Rosemary's Baby"

1968:   USA troops massacre 500 civilians at My Lai in Vietnam

1968:   Stanley Kubrick directs the film "2001 A Space Odyssey"

1968:   Martin Luther King is assassinated

1968:   520,000 USA troops are in Vietnam

1968:   Anthony Braxton, a member of the Chicago Association for the Advancement of Creative Musicians, releases his improvisations "For Alto Saxophone"

1968:   Louis Meisel founds the painting movement "Photorealism"

1968:   Philip Noyce, Gordon Moore and Andy Grov found Intel ("Integrated Electronics") to build memory chips

1968:   John Portman designs the Embarcadero Center in San Francisco

1968:   Frank Malina founds Leonardo ISAST in Paris, an organization devoted to art/science fusion

1968:   John Bryan and Bill Edwards found the investment company Bryan & Edwards

1968:   Doug Engelbart of the Stanford Research Institute demonstrates the NLS ("oN-Line System"), the first system to employ the mouse

1968:   Luis Alvarez of the Lawrence Berkeley Labs is awarded the Nobel Prize

1969:   Gary Starkweather of Xerox invents the laser printer

1969:   Frank Oppenheimer founds the San Francisco Exploratorium as a museum of science, art and human perception

1969:   Construction begins at 3000 Sand Hill Road, in Menlo Park, soon to become the headquarters of the venture-capital community

1969:   Ted Codd of IBM invents the relational database

1969:   Bell Labs unveils the Unix operating system developed by Kenneth Thompson and Dennis Ritchie

1969:   The computer network ArpaNET is inaugurated with four nodes, three of which are in California (UCLA, Stanford Research Institute and UC Santa Barbara)

1969:   Howard Wise organizes the exhibition "Television As A Creative Medium"

1969:   Charles Wuorinen composes the electronic poem "Time's Encomium"

1969:   USA astronaut Neil Armstrong becomes the first man to set foot on the Moon

1969:   A huge crowd marches on Washington to demand an end to the Vietnam war

1969:   Miles Davis invents jazz-rock

1969:   Sam Peckinpah directs the film "The Wild Bunch"

1969:   Claes Oldenburg creates the interactive sculpture "Lipstick (Ascending) on Caterpillar Tracks"

1969:   Gary Starkweather of Xerox invents the laser printer

1969:   Frank Oppenheimer founds the San Francisco Exploratorium as a museum of science, art and human perception

1969: Construction begins at 3000 Sand Hill Road, in Menlo Park, soon to become the headquarters of the venture-capital community

1969: Ted Codd of IBM invents the relational database

1969: Bell Labs unveils the Unix operating system developed by Kenneth Thompson and Dennis Ritchie

1969: The computer network ArpaNET is inaugurated with four nodes, three of which are in California (UCLA, Stanford Research Institute and UC Santa Barbara)

1969: Howard Wise organizes the exhibition "Television As A Creative Medium"

1969: Charles Wuorinen composes the electronic poem "Time's Encomium"

1969: USA astronaut Neil Armstrong becomes the first man to set foot on the Moon

1969: A huge crowd marches on Washington to demand an end to the Vietnam war

1969: Miles Davis invents jazz-rock

1969: Sam Peckinpah directs the film "The Wild Bunch"

1969: Claes Oldenburg creates the interactive sculpture "Lipstick (Ascending) on Caterpillar Tracks"

1983: Pioneer 10 becomes the first manmade object to leave the solar system

1984: "House" music comes out of Chicago

1984: The "Cirque du Soleil" is founded in Quebec by a group of street performers

1984: USA architect John Burgee builds the AT&T Building in New York

1984: The The Santa Fe Institute is founded to carry out interdisciplinary research

1984: Cisco is founded by Leonard Bosack and Sandra Lerner

1984: Robert Gaskins and Dennis Austin develop "Presentation", an application to create slide presentations (later renamed "PowerPoint")

1984: The "Search For Extraterrestrial Intelligence" or SETI Institute is founded

1984: Michael McGreevy creates the first virtual-reality environment at NASA Ames

1984: Nicholas Negroponte and Jerome Wiesner found the MIT Media Lab

1984:   Wavefront introduces the first commercial 3D-graphics software

1984:   Hewlett-Packard introduces the first ink-jet printer

1984:   Apple introduces the Macintosh, which revolutionizes desktop publishing

1984:   William Gibson's novel "Neuromancer" popularizes the "cyberpunks"

1984:   The CDROM is introduced by Sony and Philips

1985:   The Nintendo Entertainment System is introduced

1985:   Richard Stallman founds the non-profit organization "Free Software Foundation" (FSF)

1985:   Richard Stallman releases a free operating system, "GNU"

1985:   Stewart Brand and Larry Brilliant create the "Whole Earth Lectronic Link" (or "WELL"), a virtual community

1985:   Warren Robinett, Scott Fisher and Michael McGreevy of NASA Ames build the "Virtual Environment Workstation" for virtual-reality research, incorporating the first dataglove and the first low-cost head-mounted display

1985:   Microsoft ships the "Windows" operating system

1985:   Jim Kimsey founds Quantum Computer Services (later renamed America Online to provide dedicated online services for personal computers)

1985:   The Arpanet is renamed Internet

1985:   Jaron Lanier founds VPL Research, the first company to sell Virtual Reality products

1986:   Apple's co-founder Steve Jobs buys Pixar, that becomes an independent film studio run by Ed Catmull

1986:   Renzo Piano builds the California Academy of Science in San Francisco

1986:   Yuan Lee of the Lawrence Berkeley Labs is awarded the Nobel Prize

1987:   Chris Langton coins the term "Artificial Life"

1987:   The JPEG (Joint Photographic Experts Group format is introduced)

1987:   Tod Machover composes the opera "Valis" with electronically processed voices

1987:   USA architect Paul Rudolph designs Hong Kong's Lippo building

1987:   The world's first conference on Artificial Life is held at the Los Alamos National Laboratory

1987: The USA writer Joseph McElroy publishes the novel "Women and Men"

1988: "Morris", the first digital worm, infects most of the Internet

1989: UC Berkeley introduces the "BSD license", one of the first open-source licences

1989: Adobe releases Photoshop

1988: Harvard University announces the first genetically engineered animal

1988: Robert Zemeckis' "Who Framed Roger Rabbit" makes live actors and animated characters interact realistically

1990: The "Human Genome Project" is launched to decipher human DNA

1990: Richard Taylor of Stanford University is awarded the Nobel Prize in Physics and William Sharpe of Stanford University is awarded the Nobel Prize in Economics

1990: Michael West founds biotech company Geron that pioneers commercial applications of regenerative medicine

1990: Tim Berners-Lee of CERN invents the HyperText Markup Language "HTML" and demonstrates the World-Wide Web

1990: The first Internet search engine, "Archie", is developed in Montreal

1990: The Hubble Space Telescope is launched

1991: The USA leads the Gulf War against Iraq, the first war to use high-precision bombs guided by the GPS

1991: John Corigliano composes the opera "Ghosts of Versailles"

1991: The first economic recession ever strikes California

1991: The World-Wide Web invented by Tim Berners-Lee in Geneve debuts on the Internet

1991: Finnish student Linus Torvalds introduces the Linux operating system, a variant of Unix

1991: Paul Lindner and Mark McCahill of the University of Minnesota release "Gopher", a software program to access the World-Wide Web

1992: Macromedia is founded in San Francisco

1992: The Electronic Visualization Lab at the University of Illinois Chicago creates a "CAVE" ("Cave Automatic Virtual Environment", a surround-screen and surround-sound virtual-reality environment (graphics projected from behind the walls that surround the user)

1992: Gary Becker of Stanford University is awarded the Nobel Prize in Economics

1992: Calgene creates the "Flavr Savr" tomato, the first genetically-engineered food to be sold in stores

1992: Apple introduces QuickTime

1992: Jean Armour Polly coins the phrase "Surfing the Internet"

1992: Thomas Ray develops "Tierra", a computer simulation of ecology

1992: The School of Visual Arts in New York launches the "New York Digital Salon"

1992: Craig Venter founds the "Institute for Genomic Research" (TIGR)

1992: Richard Baily starts his visual-effects animation company, Image Savant

1993: Stuart Kauffman publishes "The Origins of Order" that popularizes self-organizing system

1993: 88 of the 100 most viewed films of the year around the world were made in the USA

1993: The USA, Canada and Mexico sign the "North American Free Trade Agreement" (NAFTA)

993: Stanford University's professor Jim Clark hires Mark Andreesen

1993: Broderbund introduces the videogame "Myst"

1993: Adobe Systems introduces Acrobat and the file format PDF (or Portable Document Format)

1993: Marc Andreessen develops the first browser for the World Wide Web (Mosaic)

1994: The first genetically engineered vegetable (Flavr Savr tomato) is introduced

1994: DirecTV launches the first satellite-based television service

1994: Quentin Tarantino directs the film "Pulp Fiction"

1994: Richard Teitelbaum composes the interactive opera "Golem"

1994: Jerry Yang launches the first search engine, Yahoo

1994: John Harsanyi of UC Berkeley is awarded the Nobel Prize in Economics

1994: The "Band of Angels" is founded by "angels" to fund Silicon Valley start-ups

1994: University of North Carolina's college radio station WXYC becomes the first radio station in the world to broadcast its signal over the Internet

1994: Mark Pesce introduces the "Virtual Reality Modeling Language" or VRML

1994: Netscape, the company founded by Marc Andreesen, goes public even before earning money and starts the "dot.com" craze and the boom of the Nasdaq

1995: John Lasseter's "Toy Story" is the first feature-length computer-animated film

1995: Bill Gates becomes the richest man in the world

1995: The MP3 standard is introduced

1995: Mario Botta builds the Modern Museum of Art in San Francisco

1995: Martin Perl of Stanford University is awarded the Nobel Prize in Physics

1995: The Sony Playstation is introduced

1995: Ward Cunningham creates WikiWikiWeb, the first "wiki", a manual on the internet maintained in a collaborative manner

1995: SUN launches Java

1995: Piero Scaruffi debuts his website www.scaruffi.com

1995: Craig Newmark starts craigslist.com on the Internet, a regional advertising community

1995: Robert Fleischmann of the "Institute for Genomic Research" (TIGR) sequences a living organism's genome

1995: 36 million cars are manufactured in the world, of which 7.6 million in Japan and 6.3 million in the USA

1995: A right-wing extremist blows up a federal building in Oklahoma City, killing 160 people in the worst terrorist incident in the history of the USA until then

1995: Digital artist Char Davies creates the immersive virtual-reality environment "Osmose (1995)

1995: Bulgarian-born Christo Javacheff wraps the Reichstag in Berlin

1996: Bill Viola creates the video installation "The Crossing"

1996: Former BBC employees launch "Al Jazeera", the first pan-Arab satellite news channel (from Qatar)

1996: Sabeer Bhatia launches Hotmail, a website to check email from anywhere in the world

1996: Douglas Osheroff of Stanford University is awarded the Nobel Prize in Physics

1996: Macromedia introduces Flash

1996: The first DVD player is introduced by Toshiba

1996: The Apache HTTP Server is introduced, an open-source web server

1996: 1996: Monsanto acquires Calgene

1996: Stewart Brand and Danny Hillis establish the "Long Now Foundation"

1997: Amazon.com is launched on the web as the "world's largest bookstore", except that it is not a bookstore, it is a website

1997: Myron Scholes of Stanford University is awarded the Nobel Prize in Economics

1997: Steven Chu of Stanford University is awarded the Nobel Prize in Physics

1997: Evite is founded by Stanford engineering students Al Lieb and Selina Tobaccowala

1997: David Lynch directs the film "Lost Highway"

1997: Rob Silvers publishes the photographic collages "Photomosaics"

1998: Larry Page and Sergey Brin found Google to develop a search engine

1998: Saul Perlmutter's team at the Lawrence Berkeley Lab discovers that the expansion of the universe is accelerating

1998: Celera, presided by Craig Venter of "The Institute for Genomic Research" (TIGR), is established to map the human genome (and later relocated to the Bay Area)

1998: Netscape launches the open-source project "Mozilla" of Internet applications

1998: Robert Laughlin of Stanford University is awarded the Nobel Prize in Physics

1998: America Online acquires Netscape

1998: Pierre Omidyar founds Ebay, a website to trade second-hand goods

1998:   Yahoo, Amazon, Ebay and scores of Internet-related start-ups create overnight millionaires

1998:   Jorn Barger in Ohio coins the term "weblog" for webpages that simply contain links to other webpages

1998:   Bob Somerby starts "The Daily Howler", the first major political blog

1999:   Camille Utterback's "Text Rain" pioneers interactive digital art

1999:   Blogger.com allows people to create their own "blogs", or personal journals

1999:   Philip Rosedale founds Linden Lab to develop virtual-reality hardware

1999:   The world prepares for the new millennium amidst fears of computers glitches due to the change of date (Y2K)

1999:   The recording industry sues Shawn Fanning's Napster, a website that allows people to exchange music

1999:   100 new Internet companies are listed in the USA stock market

1999:   The USA has 250 billionaires, and thousands of new millionaires are created in just one year

1999:   Microsoft is worth 450 billion dollars, the most valued company in the world, even if it is many times smaller than General Motors, and Bill Gates is the world's richest man at $85 billion

1998:   Digital artist Mark Amerika creates "Grammatron", a virtual web-based environment

1999:   Eduardo Kac's "Genesis" pioneers the use of genetics as an art medium

1999:   NATO bombs Serbia to stop repression against ethnic Albanians in Kosovo

1999:   Protests disrupt the meeting of the World Trade Organization in Seattle

Made in the USA
Columbia, SC
09 November 2020

24219227R00050